T0348661

ELKE GERAERTS

FOCUS

IS THE NEW

GOLD

How to Reduce Stress and Increase
Productivity in a Distracted World

Lannoo

CONTENTS

Prologue

"I'm late! I'm late! For a very important date! No time to say hello, goodbye!" The famous White Rabbit quote from Lewis Carroll's *Alice's Adventures in Wonderland* still sounds topical today, even though the world that felt so fast and busy to Carroll in the mid-1800s is nothing compared with the way we hurtle through life in the 21st century. We have shifted up a few gears. And perhaps more importantly, we have forgotten where the off switch is.

Our clever human brain has helped us create a world we can no longer keep up with. The result? Stress, lots of it. Every day we wake up in a world where constant connectivity sets the agenda. Smartphones, social media and a relentless stream of notifications make it ever harder for us to focus on the tasks that really matter. That constant bombardment of information has the added side effect that our attention is constantly fragmented. Distraction lurks everywhere and it is difficult to focus our attention on just one thing.

Check for yourself: how full-to-bursting is *your* schedule? How many to-do's are still waiting to be ticked off? Or do you have a to-do list of to-do lists that you need to finish? They reflect the chaos in our heads: many of us are in constant overdrive and have completely lost our focus. Are *you* managing to keep up?

No wonder rates of stress and burnout are at an all-time high. The crazy thing is, we know what we need to do to stop this brain health crisis. Except our overstimulated brains seem unable to grasp that knowledge yet, let alone put it into practice. We know that plenty of sleep, regular exercise, and rest and relaxation are essential to keep us healthy and resilient, but modern life makes it hard to apply this good advice consistently. The social pressure to be available and productive anytime, anywhere, is undermining our mental health. We

I CHALLENGE YOU
TO READ
-> JUST ONE PAGE <-
WITHOUT STOPPING.

feel guilty if we don't respond instantly to messages or if we take a moment to ourselves, when in fact it's precisely these moments of rest that are crucial for our mental and emotional health.

The result is that we spend most of our lives on autopilot. Day in, day out, we perform the same actions without ever questioning them. This works fine in more predictable times, but we're currently in the throes of an unprecedented polycrisis – think pandemic, wars in Ukraine and Gaza, energy crisis, inflation and climate change. We can no longer afford to cling to the past. To echo the lyrics of a classic from the music archives: "The times they are a changin'." Those who remain passive will be left behind. Those who seize control of their lives will be the winners.

It's more important than ever to actively increase our focus and resilience. And we *can* do that: our brain has a lot to deal with, but it's also much more resilient than we think. The key to success? Understanding how your brain works, so you can make the targeted adjustments you need. So you can stop feeling as if your life is being lived for you, and can actively choose what to focus on and when.

That is the purpose of this book. My aim is to help you identify what keeps hijacking your focus and then equip you with the tools you need to regain that focus. Are you ready?

CHAPTER 1

WHY WE ARE ALL PIGEONS

"ARE YOU READY?"

In spring 2024 during a busy week of lecturing, I was settling down for a lovely al fresco lunch in London's Covent Garden when a striking scene caught my attention. For anyone who's never been, Covent Garden is a melting pot of activity where people of all ages and backgrounds come together under the inviting canopies of trendy little boutiques and hip eateries.

I watched a street performer take to the central stage in the piazza. Noticing the charismatic figure, a number of passers-by stopped in their tracks. Then, without much further ado, he launched smoothly into his act. The handful of onlookers soon mushroomed into a small crowd. It was as if they were all bound together by a secret agreement: to be in that place at that time to see that performer at work, which, of course, was not the case. The scene that played out in front of me was fascinating because most of the onlookers remained stock-still. They didn't want to miss a single second of the show. There was a tangible sense of FOMO, fear of missing out.

"Are you ready?" The performer's commanding voice rang through the crowd like a mantra, compelling them to focus on the spectacle. He captured the attention of everyone in the piazza. And he held it: as his act continued, he strengthened his grip on the crowd, like a conductor blending hundreds of voices and hands into a harmonious whole. The audience's enthusiasm grew to a crescendo and was translated into enormous generosity after the performer's final bow. The hat on the ground in front of him quickly filled up with donations.

But it wasn't just him: almost every performer who followed him – and who also had twenty minutes to do their thing – succeeded in capturing the audience's attention. Each of them held the audience in the palm of their hand for twenty whole minutes. No one got distracted. Yes, a few smartphones were fished out, but only to capture this unique moment, not to disappear down some rabbit hole of breaking news.

As I watched the show, I saw it as a brilliant allegory for focus and engagement, in sharp contrast with the constant distractions of our modern lives. Because that's how we now manoeuvre through our day: though we have work to do, we are constantly having to fend off distractions lurking just around the corner, whispering in our ear that we've earned a short break.

A PERFECT DAY

Imagine you wake up one morning and feel completely rested. The total relaxation you had last night led to an invigorating sleep, so you can start today's to-do list full of energy. You get into the flow right away, and it's lunchtime before you know it. In normal circumstances, the work you've done over the past few hours would have taken you two days. But today? You're flying through it. In the evening, you're still bursting with energy. You decide to go for a 5K run and then chill out by cooking a nice meal.

Wouldn't it be great to look back on an almost perfect day? Unfortunately, for many people, it's a scenario they can scarcely imagine. How often do *you* feel you can work with 100% focus? We live in a world where our attention spans are under increasing pressure. A new distraction lurks around every corner. The result? At the end of the day, we feel we haven't even achieved all that much, and yet we're tired. Dead tired.

How did it come to this point, where our focus and attention are getting weaker every year? Where we can barely read even one page of a book any more without reaching for our smartphones? Over the last two decades, we've trained our brain to give in continuously to all sorts of internal and external impulses. And every year that distraction grows, like an unstoppable snowball rolling down a mountainside, getting bigger and bigger.

THE TEMPTATION OF DISTRACTION

In his bestseller *Hooked. How to Build Habit-Forming Products*, Israeli-American author Nir Eyal introduces a technique to help companies create products and services that tap into the psychology of habits. If your company can get people addicted to its products, you will retain customers more easily. This opens the way to faster growth and bigger profits: for example, you'll be able to be much more creative and flexible with your pricing. Why is that? Customers who are already hooked on your product are less sensitive to price changes.

Translating this to our modern-day smartphone usage, it's clear that many people are not afraid to dig deep into their pockets every time a big phone brand releases a new model. The app developers too do their utmost to keep their users as tied in as possible. And it works: we scroll like mad, often sharing our personal data without thinking, so companies can keep refining their already clever apps and control our behaviour even more. We arrange our lives to suit the delusion of the latest apps: we are all connected, but often no longer with each other.

What makes Eyal's story remarkable is the fact that he wrote a second book, *Indistractable. How to Control Your Attention and Choose Your Life*, in which – ironically – he aims to help people distance themselves from the distractions they are addicted to, so they can take back control of their own lives.

First tell companies how to engage consumers more easily, then write a book for consumers on how to win that battle for attention and distraction for themselves? Is this some carefully crafted master plan? No, Eyal is genuinely concerned about the devastating impact that smartphones, apps and social media are having on our attention span. In a world full of devices angling for our attention by sending notifications every five minutes, it seems only logical that we should lose control. Haven't you ever thought: I could have spent this hour much more usefully rather than sitting here scrolling aimlessly on my phone.

Luckily, we are not powerless, says Eyal. Our main weapon in the battle for our attention is understanding how big tech companies exploit the way our brains work. Facebook and co. know all too well that we humans are easy prey when we feel boredom, stress or some other discomfort. We go looking for distractions. An endless stream of TikTok reels? Our brain likes nothing better: it stops us having to think about difficult things.

According to Eyal, the first and most important thing to do is to identify our own internal triggers. When do you seek distraction? When do you get bored? What stresses you out? Only when you know your internal triggers can you start looking for strategies to tackle them differently.

That's what we're going to do in this book. I want to explain to you how the brain works and then explore together how to train your attention muscle in a targeted way. So that, even in this distracted world, you can get back in control of your own life and find your focus.

WE'RE JUST PIGEONS TOO

In my lectures, when talking about distraction and how human beings are constantly on the lookout for new input, I often cite the pigeon experiment conducted by American psychologist B.F. Skinner. Because make no mistake: we too are just pigeons pecking away at random.

Skinner isolated a pigeon in a chamber (the Skinner Box) that also contained a push-button. When the pigeon pressed the button, it received a reward. We call this operant conditioning or positive reinforcement: something for something, a quid pro quo. Interestingly, when the reward was variable and unpredictable, the pigeon pressed the button much more often. You never know if something else might be coming. Just as we keep doggedly pressing the send-and-receive button or refreshing the news feed in our favourite app over and over, to be sure not to miss a single post.

Follow the algorithm

You've probably experienced this too: you watch an entertaining clip in your Instagram feed and, before you realise it, you've suddenly lost an hour. How is it that you get sucked into that whirlpool of content? It's the algorithms that get you every time.

Notifications. Algorithms keep your smartphone constantly sending out a volley of notifications. A new email? A friend who's liked your photo? A post on your community app? Breaking news? Bang: four fresh notifications on your screen, each with or without an accompanying ping.

Content personalisation. How does Instagram know what you want to see? Why does a search lead to the same sites over and over? Algorithms! They're like super-spies that customise the content we are shown, based on our preferences, interests and behaviours. Yes, this can help us find relevant information, but it also means we get distracted by interesting but non-urgent 'must-reads', 'you-need-to-see-this! videos' or 'super-cute posts' and so linger on social media for much longer than we want to. The same goes for Netflix and other streaming services: you've only just finished binge-watching one series when a suggestion pops up for the next.

Social interactions. Algorithms are great at filtering and foregrounding social interactions on social media and messaging apps. Platforms like Facebook, Instagram and TikTok are designed to draw us in deeper and deeper. 'Oh, an interesting post!' Before you know it, you're scrolling through all the comments and joining in the discussion. Then you check back every ten minutes to see if anyone's responded to your comment.

SCROLLING PIGEONS

We're no cleverer than Skinner's pigeons: our brain, just like theirs, is guided by punishments and rewards. Gamification elements in apps use the principle of operant conditioning to motivate users to perform certain actions more and more often. Unlocking the next level in a game, the Duolingo owl that urges you on to one more language lesson, apps where you collect various tokens or virtual currencies: these are all rewards that encourage you to spend even more time in a game or app. Not all of this is negative, by any means: there are also many apps these days that help us to live healthier lives. Think

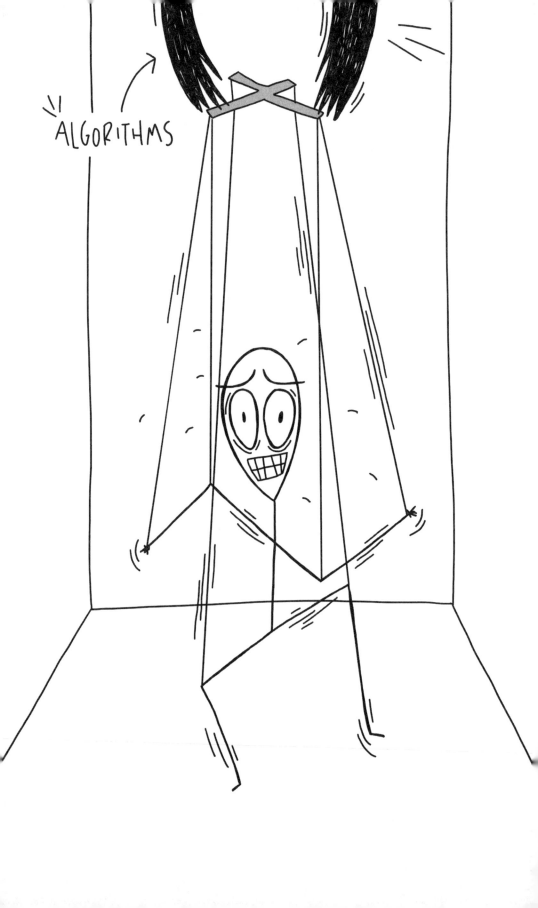

of fitness apps that reward you when you've walked a certain number of steps or drunk enough water: some of these can definitely help you to be more active and healthier in life.

But there's no escaping the fact that all of these apps are extremely addictive. So conscious consumption is the message. If that little Duolingo owl helps you express yourself a bit more fluently while holidaying on the French Riviera, I certainly wouldn't stop you. But if you notice you're all too easily losing an hour on it every day, it might make sense to find a different way to learn a language.

The crazy thing is, we all know how addictive social media can be. But we still keep falling into the traps laid by various apps, only to realise to our disappointment after wandering for an hour that we've already lost precious time we could have spent a lot more usefully.

HOW DOPAMINE DERAILS OUR FOCUS

Why *do* we keep scrolling against our better judgement? Because every like, share or comment we receive rewards us with a shot of dopamine. To many people, dopamine is a kind of happiness drug with an instant feel-good effect. That's not entirely right: dopamine is a neurotransmitter that is indeed often mentioned in the same breath as pleasure, but that's only part of the story. The main role of dopamine is not to make us feel pleasure, but to determine our focus. Dopamine tells us where to direct our attention. Swedish psychiatrist Anders Hansen wrote about this at length in his book *The Attention Fix: How to Focus in a World that Wants to Distract You*, and offers some fascinating insights.

For example, if you're hungry and someone puts a plate of food in front of you, dopamine levels rise in your brain. It's the dopamine that says: 'You should eat that.' Interestingly, dopamine likes uncertain rewards, probably because most rewards in nature are variable. Back in the early days of human history, if you climbed a tree in search of food, you never really knew if you'd be rewarded for that act. You might find a whole bunch of ripe fruits, or nothing at all. The same applied to hunting: there was no certainty of finding any prey, let alone outsmarting it. This might be the reason why our brains like to reward uncertain outcomes in particular.

I mentioned earlier the way that social media platforms keep luring you back. The system they use for this is entirely based on that dopamine rush. When you post a photo on Facebook and your friends give you a thumbs up, you don't see the likes all at once. Facebook spreads them out, to keep you coming back to see if there's anything new. Basically, your smartphone is a sort of gambling den that shows you every so often how many 'likes' you have won. This is just one of the many ways that tech companies capture our attention. Especially for companies like Meta, our attention is the world's most valuable commodity.

It's precisely because our phones raise dopamine levels in our brains so incredibly efficiently that they monopolise our attention. The outside world can't compete with this: it doesn't give us so many dopamine shots. American psychologist Larry Rosen researches the dynamics of the modern brain, especially in relation to our interactions with media and technology. He found that constantly checking smartphones and navigating between different media activities triggers the same reward circuits in the brain as drug use. This can lead to a kind of addiction to technology, with young people becoming increasingly dependent on constant stimulation and finding it hard to concentrate on a single task.

The consequences should not be underestimated. Even when we're not actively using our device, it still divides our attention. In some fascinating studies, for example, students were asked to complete a test designed to gauge their focus and memory. At the start of the test, half of them left their smartphones outside the room. And what was the outcome? The students without phones performed better than those who had one with them, even if it just stayed unused in their pocket. The reason may be that a smartphone is so addictive and delivers so much dopamine that the constant need to suppress the impulse not to pick the thing up reduces our mental capacity.

It's no wonder then – despite the constant dopamine hits that are supposed to make us feel good – that we've quietly developed a love-hate relationship with our phones. For example, in an experiment in which people talked to a stranger for ten minutes, participants reported that they found the conversation less interesting if there was a smartphone on the table. And they also considered the other person less trustworthy. A notebook proved much less intrusive. This experiment nicely illustrates the way that our digital devices reduce our interest in other people and can even make us suspicious of them.

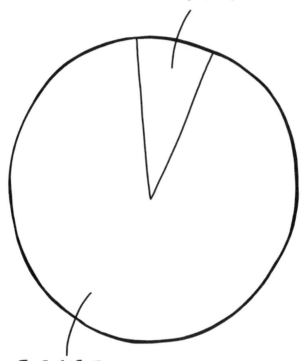

TIME SPENT
VIEWING
CONTENT

TIME SPENT
REFRESHING
REFRESHING
REFRESHING, BECAUSE
YOU NEVER KNOW
WHENANEWMESSAGEWILLBEPOSTEDONLINE!!/!!/

ONE REWARD IS NOT LIKE ANOTHER

It will be clear to you by now that, just like Skinner's pigeons, we humans hop from one reward to another. But some rewards are a lot more addictive than others. For a better understanding of why we are all collectively so hooked, I'd like to tell you a bit more about four different types of reward.

1 *The reward comes according to a fixed schedule*
   (fixed interval reinforcement)
   In fixed interval reinforcement, behaviour is rewarded after a specified amount of time has elapsed. Say Peter is having surgery and needs pain relief during his recovery. His doctor sets a limit of one dose per hour. Peter receives his medication by intravenous infusion. Because the reward (pain relief) is given at a fixed interval, there's no point in pressing the button more often.

2 *The reward comes after an unpredictable amount of time has*
   elapsed (variable interval reinforcement)
   In variable interval reinforcement, rewards are given based on time periods that are both varying and unpredictable. Take Carla, the manager of a fast food restaurant. Once in a while, a quality inspector visits. If the restaurant is clean and the service is fast, all of the staff earn a bonus. Carla doesn't know when they will be inspected, so she keeps motivating her team to provide consistently good service.

3 *The reward comes after a specified number of correct responses (fixed-ratio reinforcement)*

Fixed-ratio reinforcement rewards behaviour after a specified number of responses. Hakim works in an eyewear shop where he earns a commission on every pair of glasses sold. So his main aim is to sell as many pairs as possible, regardless of whether or not his customers really need them. The quality of what he sells doesn't matter because his commission is based purely on the number of pairs sold.

4 *The reward comes after a random number of correct responses (variable-ratio reinforcement)*

In variable-ratio reinforcement, the number of responses required for a reward varies. This type of reward is the most addictive. Let's take the example of Sarah, who is on a dream trip around the Western USA and is spending an evening in Las Vegas. Sarah has never gambled before, but now that she's in Vegas, she wants to know what all the fuss is about. She feeds a quarter into a slot machine, and another, and another. Nothing happens. After two dollars' worth of quarters, her curiosity has faded: how boring is this? 'One more quarter, then I'll go for a snack.' Suddenly the machine lights up, bells start to ring and a flood of quarters spews out. This looks more like it. With renewed interest, she feeds more coins into the machine. A few minutes later, she's already five dollars down. Maybe it's best to stop now, she thinks. But she keeps on feeding coins into the slot. Who knows, maybe one more quarter will make up her losses, and it might even deliver a jackpot…

YOUR SMARTPHONE:
A POCKET-SIZED CASINO

Gambling is so addictive because it is based on variable-ratio reinforcement: players keep trying and hoping for that big win because the reward is never predictable. You could win at any time. (The fact that most times you lose is something our brains conveniently forget.)

You've probably guessed it: the apps in our smartphones take cunning advantage of that same variable-ratio reward system. Just like a casino, social media platforms such as Facebook and Instagram offer an unpredictable stream of rewards. Only it's not about tinkling coins, but shots of dopamine. It's this thrilling uncertainty that makes social media so attractive and engaging. Just as you don't know when a gamble will win the jackpot, you never know exactly when you'll create that one post that goes viral or be inundated with a flood of likes. This is precisely what holds our brains hostage, making us constantly crave the next shot of appreciation. So we keep scrolling and clicking. Think of it as an exciting adventure where every swipe brings an opportunity for surprise and reward. The variable-ratio reward system makes us constantly crave more, seeking the next moment of digital triumph.

ALL THIS SWIPING IS MAKING US SICK

Starting to feel a bit concerned? So you should be! It's high time we recognised the impact that smartphones and social media have on our brains and our lives. I'm thinking in particular of the whole generation of young people who are learning to swipe and like from childhood. I certainly wouldn't want to stand around waving a reproachful finger, but I also feel it's my duty as a neuropsychologist to get up on the barricades to protect our children and young people. It's true, however, that you can't really make pronouncements about a new technology until it has been the subject of long-term research. Smartphones and social media are still relatively new, so we don't yet have a body of data to take as our basis. So we can't yet say with precision what the impact is on the brains of children and young adults, or how their development is being disrupted. But the alarm bells are ringing ever louder.

Globally, we are seeing an increase in suicides, depression, anxiety disorders and self-harm among young people. The origin of this increase can be pinpointed to 2012, the year the smartphone debuted on the world stage. Coincidence? Not according to American psychologist Jonathan Haidt. In his recent book *The Anxious Generation*, he highlights the impact of smartphones on young people's everyday lives and development. He argues that constant access to the internet has changed young people's experiences and developmental paths in various areas, such as friendship, relationships, sexuality, school and identity. As many as 20% of 11- to 18-year-olds feel unhappy several times a week. You'd almost be tempted to take away your child's smartphone right now. And you're not alone: take a look at the documentary *The Social Dilemma*, for example. At one point Tristan Harris, a former product manager at Google and co-founder of the Center for Humane Technology, comments that many people in the tech industry keep their children well away from smartphones. They know all too well how addictive and dangerous their own creations are. Alex Roetter, a former Vice President of Engineering at Twitter, doesn't let his kids use social media. "That's a rule." Tim Kendall, a former top executive at Facebook and Pinterest, is even more adamant: "We are zealots about it. And we don't let our kids have really any screen time."

As someone said to me recently, "this is the biggest-ever uncontrolled experiment on the brains of our adolescents." Of course, more research is still needed into the effects of social media on our brain, but does that mean in the interim that we'll keep watching from the sidelines until it's too late? We know what we need to do to make social media safe for our children. It's time for us – and by extension the tech industry – to actually start doing something with that knowledge. Our children's well-being is at stake.

Never before have there been so many young people on a psychologist's or psychiatrist's waiting list. The smartphone is not the only culprit, of course: that would be an oversimplification. We live in complex times, where the resilience of our young people is under pressure on various fronts. Think of the high rates of divorce and relationship breakdown, for example, depriving young people of a happy home. The COVID epidemic inflicted deep wounds and the ongoing crises – Gaza, Ukraine, climate change – have soured many people's view of the future. We live in "liquid times", as Polish sociologist Zygmunt Bauman so aptly put it. Recent decades have seen us swept up in a culture of temptation and marketing. Everything has to be special and the ordinary is deadly dull. Isn't it fun to browse around concept stores while sipping a latte cinnamon macchiato frappé, checking out the latest trendy fashion brands, buying organic seeds and maybe squeezing in a cheeky shiatsu massage? Admit it, who wouldn't enjoy that? But the ordinary everyday? We've lost that. If we get even a whiff of boredom, we've forgotten how to deal with it. Being bored is no longer allowed, even though it's healthy for our brain to do nothing sometimes. Nowadays we constantly seek instant gratification. Everything has to be right now, this minute.

Children – and their parents – face huge challenges. Being smarter and more critical in our interactions with new technologies is by no means the only solution, but I believe it to be an incredibly important part of the puzzle.

Is banning better?

Should we limit smartphone use during school hours? The short answer is yes! For example, the Norwegian Institute of Public Health showed that banning smartphones at school has a positive effect, especially among girls. A phone ban not only improved their school results but also led to a marked drop in mental health issues. Among both boys and girls, there was also a significant decrease in bullying behaviour.

We really shouldn't underestimate the impact of smartphones on the brains of growing children and adolescents. The education sector shares my concerns. Many schools have already introduced phone bans during lessons and some are gradually extending these bans to break times and other parts of the school day. Opponents argue that smartphones are simply part of young people's lives. So is banning them such a good idea? Isn't it better to allow smartphones in schools, so you can teach young people to use them in a healthy way? Because even if you ban a phone at school, the thing will inevitably come out again as soon as classes are over.

Speaking from my background in neuropsychology, I want to be clear: smartphones and learning do not mix. Schools that ban phones from the classroom have my full support. Of course, schools have little or no impact on what students do outside the classroom. Simply limiting screen time is not enough by itself. I believe the most important thing we can do is to make children and young people aware of how harmful overuse can be. And if we also offer concrete tools that help them to break bad habits – such as responding on impulse to messages – we may be able to really help young people find a healthy balance in their online habits. The Better Minds at School foundation hopes to make as many young people, parents and teachers as possible aware of smart ways to use your brain.

Smartphones and tablets are not only dangerous due to their direct effects; they also cause us to do less of other things. For example, today's children and adolescents spend less time engaged in physical play. Even though it's crucial for their development. Romping around outdoors, climbing trees and learning to judge which branch is safe and which isn't, playing board games together... These are all valuable forms of physical play that help children expand their motor and social skills. Physical play helps them overcome fears, gauge risks more accurately and work together, which makes them better prepared to face bigger challenges later on.

I hear some parents boast that their child could swipe before they could crawl. But is that really something to be proud of? Children have what is called a 'scouting system'. So do adults, but it's mostly children who use it to explore, discover and learn. It's their way of building a picture of the world. If a child just sits swiping away on a screen, that system isn't really stimulated in any way.

According to the international PISA survey, the educational performance of pupils in European schools is deteriorating sharply. Reading proficiency scores have been falling at ever faster rates since 2015. Reading comprehension is getting worse. The shrinking attention spans of our children and adolescents undoubtedly play a major role in this. "The crux of the matter," according to neuropsychiatrist Theo Compernolle in a recent interview, "is that our brain can only pay attention to one thing at a time. If we're constantly distracted by our phones, that becomes impossible and our brain becomes scrambled. In order to learn well, we need to pay sustained attention. A ban is vital."

The virtual world also eats up time at the expense of social relationships. Compared to 2010, young people now spend almost an hour less every day physically interacting with their friends. Yes, they do compensate with virtual interaction, but is that equally valuable? In virtual communication, spontaneous reactions and body language are lost, which can lead to misunderstandings. You've probably experienced a chat that went off the rails because you or the other person misinterpreted something. Virtual communication is also more non-committal. Don't feel like talking any more? Then just stop talking. Not keen on a relationship any more? Then quit it or, worse, ghost them. Relationships start to become disposable.

Focus in and on the Amazon rainforest

The world doesn't stand still and the technological revolution is finding its way to the most inaccessible places on the planet. One story I want to share with you is that of the Marubo people. This community has co-existed in harmony with nature for centuries, living in communal huts scattered along the banks of the Ituí River deep in the Amazon rainforest. Its members speak their own language, take ayahuasca to connect with the forest spirits, and catch spider monkeys for the pot or to keep as pets. By isolating themselves from the outside world, the Marubo have preserved their way of life for generations. Some villages take more than a week to reach.

But a few years ago, everything changed. This time it wasn't illegal loggers that turned the Marubo's life upside down, but Starlink, the satellite internet project operated by Elon Musk's SpaceX. Since Starlink was introduced in Brazil in 2022, the internet has arrived in one of the last offline areas on Earth, deep in the world's largest rainforest. And that has had its consequences. According to the village elders, at first everyone was delighted: the internet allowed video chats with far-away family members and facilitated distress calls in an emergency. It's only now, two years later, that

the negative impact of the internet is becoming clear. Young people are getting lazy, losing interest in traditions and spending too much time online, seeing things that are at odds with the values and norms of the community.

Today the Marubo experience the same problems that have plagued North American households for years: teenagers glued to their phones, gossipy group chats, addictive social networks, violent video games, scams, misinformation and minors viewing pornography. This immediately raises an important question: how can a community maintain its focus in a world full of digital distractions? The Marubo, who have always nurtured a deeper connection with their environment and with each other, now need to navigate the challenges of the modern internet.

Sudden access to the internet is changing the way the Marubo focus on their traditional activities. Young people who used to spend time learning the old crafts are now more inclined to spend time on their phones. The focus is shifting from tangible cultural skills to fleeting digital interactions. And going back to a time pre-internet isn't an option. But that poses a major challenge: how do you retain the positive aspects of technological progress without losing the core values and traditions of your culture? Striking a balance between these new realities and traditional lifestyles is crucial.

For the Marubo, and many other indigenous communities, the future means integrating technology in a way that respects and preserves their unique culture and traditions. The skill is to use technology as a tool to strengthen the community without losing focus on their cultural roots.

TAKING BRAINPOWER TO THE NEXT LEVEL

You're probably thinking: I grew up without a smartphone. My brain was allowed to develop undisturbed, so my focus is probably still fine. Afraid I have to disappoint you: even for adults, there is still work to be done.

"Harder, Better, Faster, Stronger", goes the song by Daft Punk. I think it should be "Harder, Worse, Faster, Weaker". Admittedly, it doesn't sound as good, but it's the truth. If you were to deposit someone who grew up in the 1930s at a road junction in modern-day Berlin or Amsterdam, they'd be shocked at how much faster everything goes. I'm not just talking about the cars and e-bikes whizzing past or the digital advertising boards changing images every five seconds. It's not just the technology around us that has shifted up a gear. In many respects, so have we.

Researchers at the University of Maryland conducted an in-depth analysis of speeches given by US presidential candidates from 1910 to 1980. In a fascinating discovery, they found that the pace of speech had increased steadily over that period, suggesting that our cultural norms around communication have evolved over the years. Speakers try to squeeze more information into a shorter timeframe in order to hold the audience's attention. And it's not only presidential candidates who are speaking faster. The renowned journal *Language and Communication* published a study comparing the speech rates of TV presenters from the 1970s with those of today. The results were extraordinary: modern presenters speak significantly faster than their predecessors, suggesting that our modern world places a greater emphasis on speed and efficiency, even in everyday communication.

Not only are we speaking faster, we are also walking faster than before. A recent study published in *PLOS ONE* analysed the walking speeds of pedestrians in various cities over a period of several decades. The findings were astonishing: people in urban environments are walking on average 10% faster than 20 years ago.

Why is that? Changes in urban infrastructure, the advent of wearable technologies, and the culture of haste and urgency that characterises our modern society.

Our world is evolving at lightning speed and our brain can't keep pace. Just think of the volume of information we all have to process every day. So isn't it a good thing that we now have much easier access to all kinds of data? Yes, of course. For example, it's become a lot easier for me as a researcher to stay up-to-date with the latest findings of my fellow scientists. But can I process all of those updates? That's a different question.

Let's go back for a moment to the year 1986. There were no mobile phones or World Wide Web back then, let alone smartphones. In that year, the volume of information processed daily by the average individual was equivalent to the content of 40 newspapers. We're talking here about information that came to us through television, radio and written sources such as newspapers and magazines. This information comprised a broad range of topics, from news and current affairs to entertainment and personal interests. By 2007, it had grown exponentially: the volume of information processed daily by the average individual was now equivalent to the content of 174 newspapers. Besides the traditional media channels mentioned above, by 2007 we also had to digest information from emerging new technologies such as the internet and digital media. People were getting ever more and easier access to a wealth of information sources. Click, click, click, and before you knew it you were browsing the newspaper archives of a township in New Zealand.

I wouldn't dare put a figure on how many newspapers' worth we have to process nowadays. People who spend a lot of time online become overwhelmed by a stream of short information bursts. Known as 'information overload' or 'infobesity', this state leaves no room for deep reflection. It's like drinking from a fire hydrant: we are drowning in information. And what really worries me in this is that every process that takes time and attention, such as building friendships, conducting thorough research or developing empathy, is compromised as a result. Our brain simply can't cope with this constant flow of information. And that's only natural: the human brain is a powerful machine that has remained virtually unchanged for millennia. It evolved to thrive in a world full of challenges such as hunting, communicating and problem-solving. But now, in what seems like the blink of an eye, we find ourselves dealing with a completely new environment full of digital stimuli and constant distractions. We live in a jungle of smartphones, social media and endless notifications that present our primal brain with a challenge it wasn't actually made for and isn't prepared for either. The result? We often feel overwhelmed and stressed, and struggle to maintain our focus.

But there's good news too: you're not doomed to be a slave to digital distractions forever. By becoming aware of how your brain works and applying strategies geared to its natural abilities, you can improve your focus and concentration. I look at this in more detail in the following chapters.

Screen on, let's drive

Sometimes we know that things aren't good for us, but we need a little additional incentive to really accept it as true. Such as using your smartphone while driving. How often do you see people trundling along in the middle lane while fiddling with their smartphones? Every time I see one of them driving by, I'm tempted to shout: don't do that! Because it's really unsafe. My feeling on this is backed up by research by David Strayer of the University of Utah, who has extensively documented the effects of distracted driving. Strayer used sophisticated driving simulators to study subjects' behaviour during exposure to various forms of distraction, such as receiving text messages or checking their smartphones.

His research revealed that even simple tasks, such as reading a text message, can have significant effects on driving ability. Reaction times were slower and concentration was impaired. The risk of an accident was therefore much higher when subjects were distracted by technology while driving. The degree of deterioration in driving ability was similar to that of drivers under the influence of alcohol.

Distraction due to technology poses an incredibly high risk to road safety. One in five accidents today is thought to be due to distractions caused by smartphone use. But we already knew that, didn't we?

NO FOCUS WITHOUT SLEEP

I certainly wouldn't argue that everything was better in the old days, but human beings did seem to have more time to just be... human. British journalist Johann Hari talks about this at length in his book *Stolen Focus: Why You Can't Pay Attention* and offers some fascinating insights. For example, Hari talks about the fact that we now sleep 20% less on average than we did a century ago. Children are getting an estimated 85 minutes less sleep per night than they used to. It's an unsettling trend.

Some people claim that sleep is overrated, declaring that they'll "sleep when they're dead". It's high time to lay these myths to rest once and for all. The importance of sleep cannot be overestimated: no sleep, no focus. Getting by on minimal sleep is still something of a status symbol for many people, despite its inherent inefficiency. A good manager doesn't perform better on less sleep – quite the contrary. In the same way as a student won't get a better exam mark if they've pulled an all-nighter. You've probably noticed yourself how a poor night's sleep holds you hostage the following day. Even dousing your head under the cold tap or guzzling gallons of coffee doesn't really wake you up. The only thing that helps is sleep itself, which you obviously can't do while you're at work, unless there's a decompression space somewhere that you can retreat to for a post-lunch siesta.

But there's more. Sleep deprivation doesn't just eat away at our focus and concentration. Lack of sleep is downright unhealthy. So it's important to get a good night's rest. But it turns out we're nowhere near achieving that: a whopping 23% of Americans sleep for less than five hours a night, a figure that is accompanied by another worrying statistic. Barely 15% of people report feeling well-rested in the morning. As many as 40% of Americans suffer from chronic sleep deprivation. With inevitable consequences: according to Hari, chronic sleep deprivation leads to reduced cognitive performance, greater irritability, mood disorders and a higher risk of health problems.

Lack of sleep has underappreciated consequences. We may *think* we can shave a few hours off our sleep, but our bodies know better. If we don't sleep for long enough, our body interprets this as meaning that we're not resting enough because an emergency is coming. With the result that our clever brain and body go into a state of alertness in order to cope with the imminent crisis. A lack of sleep triggers several psychological processes in our brains that prepare us for major calamities.

One of these processes is increased production of stress hormones such as cortisol, which in turn has various negative effects on your body and mind. Your blood pressure rises and you crave fast food and quick sugars for a sudden energy boost so you can run away. And so on. Your body is in a state of high alert, even though there may be nothing going on. There's no crisis looming, but your body thinks there is. Your brain doesn't differentiate between not sleeping because there's a wolf on the prowl and not sleeping because you've been binge-watching that new series into the small hours of the morning. Sleep deprivation is sleep deprivation, with disastrous consequences.

When you're lacking sleep, it feels as if your mental sharpness goes into free fall. In the short term, you struggle to concentrate, your reactions are sluggish and you feel like you're navigating through a thick mental fog. Worse than that, lack of sleep not only undermines your short-term focus but also has devastating effects on your long-term mental agility. Examples include memory problems, reduced learning capacity and even an increased risk of serious neurological disorders.

Lack of sleep can affect your mood, make you prone to mood swings and send you into a vicious cycle of stress and mental exhaustion. If you want to maintain that super-strong focus and sharp mind, getting enough sleep isn't a luxury. It's an absolute necessity. Our brains need sleep in order to recover and to flush out the waste products that build up during the day. If you stay awake for 19 hours in a row, for example, your concentration is on a par with that of someone who's drunk too much and isn't safe to drive, according to Matthew Walker, professor of neuroscience and psychology at the University of California, Berkeley, in his book *Why We Sleep: The New Science of Sleep and Dreams*. Your brain still seems active, but in fact parts of it have already switched off.

Why are we sleeping less? Stress, mainly. But also because we always want to be contactable, including for work. In the past, only certain people in certain professions – think doctors or firefighters – were always on call. Nowadays, it seems as if nearly all of us have to be on standby all the time, not only during the week, but also at weekends and even on holiday. We think we'll get more work done that way, but nothing could be further from the truth.

SLEEP IS THE MIRROR OF YOUR DAY

The busyness of the day is reflected in the quality of your sleep. If you've been on the go all day, you can't expect that 'daily stress' to just disappear from your system in the evening. It lingers in your body, making it harder for you to fall asleep. And even when you do drop off, your sleep is often restless and you'll wake up several times during the night. As a result, you don't feel rested when your alarm goes off.

Want to wake up feeling refreshed and energised? Then it's a good idea to divide your day up with breaks, even if they only last a few minutes. When you take a coffee break, keep the conversation light and don't talk about work. That isn't relaxing. If you can't find a colleague to take a break with, step outside for some fresh air. Even a few minutes is enough to recharge your batteries a little.

At lunchtime, don't eat at your desk, because that doesn't count as a break. It's important to actually step away from your workstation. Be creative with your breaks. For example, take a minute's rest on the toilet to focus on your breathing and cut yourself off from the outside world for a while. Or put a piece of fruit on your desk as a reminder to take a break.

Turn everyday activities into moments of rest. In the car? Sing along with your favourite tunes or listen to an inspiring podcast. Every activity offers opportunities for a mini-relaxation. Find it hard to schedule breaks? Set an alarm. When it goes off, you'll know it's time to take a break.

By taking regular short breaks, you can reduce stress and improve your sleep. If you allow yourself that rest, you'll notice you feel better during the day and sleep better at night.

Back to basics: a healthy brain in a healthy body

We all know what we need to do to keep our bodies – and our brains – healthy. And yet I see many people tossing these basic rules overboard. So yes, I know it's not rocket science and you've probably heard the following advice umpteen times. But if it's not rocket science, why aren't we doing it?

1 **Sleep.** A good night's rest is vital for our cognitive function and overall health. Scientists recommend sleeping between seven and nine hours a night to give the brain sufficient rest and allow it to run through the neural processes that are essential for memory, concentration and creativity. During sleep we consolidate memories and strengthen neural connections, making information more easily accessible. Lack of sleep can lead to forgetfulness, reduced alertness and poorer performance during the day.
2 **Exercise.** Regular exercise benefits not only our physical well-being, but also our cognitive function. It improves blood flow to the brain, enhancing mental alertness and concentration. Exercise also helps us to manage emotions and set

priorities so we can be more productive. The effects of exercise on the brain remain noticeable for several hours afterwards, which makes it a powerful way to keep our minds sharp. So make sure you fit in enough bouts of exercise. Go for a 15-minute walk, do some stretches or yoga in a spare moment, and take the stairs more often.

3 **Drink plenty of water and eat a balanced diet.** Drinking plenty of water is essential for good cognitive function and overall health. Studies have shown that even mild dehydration can lead to impaired concentration, lower thinking capacity and reduced muscle function. So it's important to drink plenty of water, especially during tasks that require a high degree of concentration. Avoiding too many sugary drinks and unhealthy foods can also help to maintain mental clarity and improve overall focus.

4 **Prioritise social connections.** Humans are social animals. There are exceptions of course, but most of us need social contact. Social relationships not only provide emotional support but also improve our well-being and can even boost our physical health. Yes, it does take time to build and maintain a strong social network, but the benefits are not to be underestimated. Social relationships at work promote a positive working environment, improve team dynamics and can even heighten productivity and focus. But it's important to respect your colleagues' boundaries. Not everyone wants the same extent of social interaction, so be aware of other people's comfort zones. Contributing to a positive workplace culture by showing friendliness and respect can be contagious and improve the overall working environment.

TECHNOLOGY ISN'T BAD PER SE

Maybe now it seems simple: throw away our smartphones and, in a flash, our focus problem is solved. Unfortunately, our lack of focus and our addiction to distraction go deeper than that. So we shouldn't just point an accusing finger at the outside world – we also need to take a good look at ourselves and scrutinise our own behaviour.

It's an open door, but I'm going to kick it in anyway. Technology in itself isn't a bad thing. It's the way we use it that is bad or good. If we look at human history, there have always been things that have distracted us. Each new development makes us prick up our ears like curious meerkats and in no time at all we're on board with the latest hype. This has actually had many positive consequences.

Ever heard of the Flynn effect? It's named after James Flynn, a New Zealand philosopher who was the first person to investigate the observation that worldwide scores on IQ tests have been increasing over time. In other words, younger generations are outperforming older ones. The average IQ is increasing by around 10 points per generation. So people in 1950 scored significantly lower than today. How is that possible? The answer is complicated. Changes in education systems and better nutrition have certainly borne fruit. But our IQ is also being boosted by the emergence of new technologies, because they encourage abstract thinking skills.

I don't have a crystal ball, but it seems a pretty safe bet that technological advancement is not about to stop any time soon. New developments are following ever harder on each other's heels. While I was writing this book, for example, a new AI application came out every week. Big tech companies have announced plans to fit people with microchips in future. And so it goes on.

Many people are wary of the rise of AI and neurolink technology. Not me. I am convinced that these new technologies will bring us more convenience, comfort and efficiency. On one condition: that we use them consciously. That means thinking about how all these developments affect our focus, our willpower, our creativity and the way our brains function. We will need to strike a balance between embracing technological progress and maintaining and indeed strengthening our human values and capabilities. For example, by deliberately setting time aside for offline activities, such as personal interactions and reflection.

How AI needn't hurt the brain

In a famous study from some years ago, researchers scanned the brains of a group of aspiring London taxi drivers. Before taking to the city's streets, black cab drivers have to learn the London A-Z by heart and pass a test called 'the Knowledge'. This is no easy task, as London has somewhere between 20,000 and 30,000 streets. That's a vast amount of information. The candidates' brains were scanned twice: once before they started learning the Knowledge and a second time after taking the test. The outcome? The drivers who passed the test were found to have an enlarged hippocampus. So when I say your brain is a muscle you can train, you can take that literally. The drivers' brains had grown because they had practised a new skill intensively.

These days we allow our digital devices to perform more and more tasks that our brains used to have to do all by themselves. This is a good thing, as tasks that used to take hours are now done in minutes. But the neuroscientist in me remains a bit sceptical. Are our brains still getting enough training? I am fine with outsourcing repetitive tasks to computers. If AI means we all have to work less, I'd be the last to protest against it. But for tasks where humans do add significant value, we need to keep our brains in tip-top shape.

I'm not afraid of AI, quite the contrary. But I do subscribe to the view of American tech writer Joan Westenberg, who says that the loss of critical reflection is a far greater threat than the advance of AI. And that critical thinking starts with how we take in information. I like to cite an experiment done with museum visitors, in which some visitors took photos of the artworks while others simply looked at them. The next day, they were tested on their recall. And what was the outcome? The visitors who had taken photos remembered less of what they had seen. The same phenomenon can be observed when reading a book: when reading on a screen, less of it sinks in. If you read the exact same text in a physical book, you pick up more details and understand the context better, especially in the case of difficult texts.

Our ability to read and comprehend is deteriorating, and not just among Gen Y. We skim and scan rather than reading carefully. Technology has enabled the widespread dissemination of information, but it has also fragmented our thinking. We are inundated by noise and sensationalism, with inevitable consequences. If we can't read and understand, we can't process and absorb information. We are losing the ability to analyse thoroughly, think critically, understand different perspectives, recognise logical fallacies and weigh evidence.

No algorithm can replace human wisdom and analysis. But no algorithm will have to do that when we've thrown away a thousand years' worth of critical reading and thinking skills.

DISTRACTION IS NOTHING NEW

Let's go back for a minute to the 1950s, when the rise of comic strips was causing concern. They were said to be bad for children's attention spans and to cause serious mental health problems. Sound familiar? The comic strip in the 1950s was what smartphones and social media are today: a source of distraction. People have always looked for new ways to keep themselves busy. If there are no distractions, we just seek – or create – one ourselves.

A striking example of how much our urge for distraction pulls our strings comes from a 2014 study conducted at the University of Virginia and published in the journal *Science*. A number of test subjects were put in a room that contained an electric shock device. When the researchers left the subjects alone for a while – with nothing to do – 67% of the men and 25% of the women opted to give themselves painful electric shocks. Just to kill time. And not just once, but repeatedly.

This study gives an interesting insight into the human psyche: we would rather suffer physical pain than expose ourselves to our inner discomfort. This insight tells me a lot about how we can guard against distraction. It's not enough to throw away our smartphones or to sign up for a digital detox retreat. We'll simply find another way not to be alone with our thoughts. No, if we really want to regain our focus in a distracted world, we need first and foremost to address the psychological reasons why we seek so much distraction in the first place.

Rather than blaming technology for our personal shortcomings, we might do better to start by scrutinising our own behaviour. Yes, that takes discipline. It's certainly not easy to guard against all the ingenious ways the big tech companies devise to make you keep reaching for your smartphone. Nowadays it's easier than ever to find distractions, but we are far from powerless. It is true, though, that we need to develop new skills in order to cope with those distractions. As Nir Eyal says too, it's not just a matter of learning to deal with external triggers such as smartphone notifications. We also – and most importantly – need to learn to deal with and respond to the psychological internal triggers that tech companies exploit to their advantage. Why are we all so prone to act on these internal triggers? Is it because we no longer want to experience our own feelings?

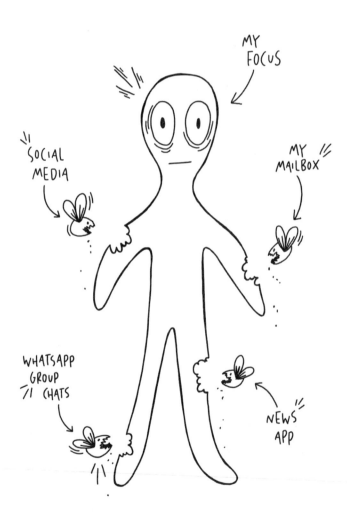

CHAPTER 2

UNFOCUSING IS THE KEY TO TRUE FOCUS

COULD WE HAVE SOME FOCUS, PLEASE?

How long can *you* concentrate on a single task? Give it a try and, despite your best intentions, you'll find it a challenge. Temptation lurks everywhere, threatening to break your concentration. A text from a friend, an email from a colleague, someone coming to you with a question, or even a beautiful butterfly fluttering against the window. Before you know it, you've been staring out the window for five minutes and your brain is running away with you.

Can you do anything about this? First the bad news: our powers of concentration peak between the ages of 30 and 40. After that, they decline with each passing year. "Youth is wasted on the young", as Irish writer George Bernard Shaw observed with perhaps a touch of hyperbole. But when it comes to focus, he is spot on: it's a pity our concentration peaks at a time in our lives when we're likely to be focused more on gaining life experiences than on acquiring knowledge.

And the good news? We can sharpen and train our focus at any time in our lives. A good way to start is by keeping an attention diary.

FIRST THE ELEPHANT

Most people keep track of their appointments and meetings in a diary, possibly combined with a to-do list. The problem is that such diaries are often decided by others: all sorts of activities creep in, and in between all those appointments you try to find time to tick off the tasks on your to-do list. Not to mention all the emails that keep arriving and expect a reply.

An attention diary is a way to proactively take matters into your own hands, planning your tasks and responsibilities based on two questions: 1) which tasks have priority? (so should definitely be fitted

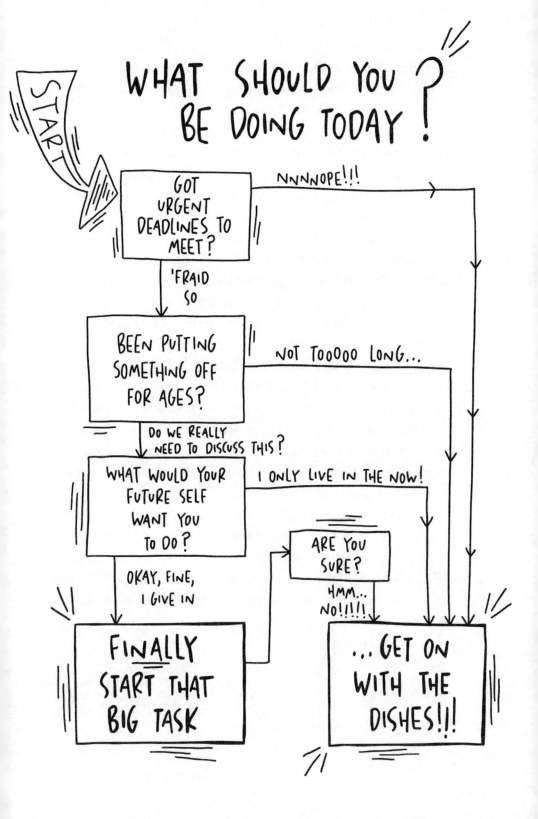

in), and 2) when is the best time to schedule those tasks? This makes it easier for you to focus on what's important and has the added benefit of making you a lot more productive.

When drawing up your attention diary, it's essential to coordinate your schedule with your natural attention peaks. So start by finding out when your natural peaks occur and plan your tasks and activities accordingly. It sounds logical to do it this way but I often see people approaching it the other way round: first they schedule the less intensive activities (such as meetings, seminars, lunches, car journeys, small to-do's) and only then do they squeeze in tasks that take a lot of concentration (like writing a report, producing an analysis or conducting an intake interview).

The main problem here is that you often do tasks that demand concentration at a time when your concentration is low. So you'll need a lot more time to complete those tasks. A less attention-intensive task – say an informal meeting or cleaning up your inbox – doesn't take much longer when you do it with less concentration. In the worst-case scenario, it might be a little harder and you might not get your views, arguments or ideas across quite so eloquently, but in general I dare say you'd do it more or less equally well at any time of the day or week.

If you ignore your natural attention peaks, you'll almost inevitably run out of time for the more important tasks. So, when drawing up your attention diary, start by mapping out your personal peaks and schedule your most demanding activities to coincide with those times. I call these tasks the 'elephants of the day': the big tasks that absolutely must be completed.

START TO ~~RUN~~ CONCENTRATE

DAY 1 — 1 × 5 MIN

DAY 2 — 2 × 5 MIN

DAY 3 — 2 × 5 MIN

DAY 4 — 2 × 10 MIN

DAY 5 — 1 × 20 MIN

DAY 6 — REST

DAY 7 — 1 × 20 MIN

DAY 8 — 1 × 25 MIN

FOCUS NEEDS TO BE TRAINED

Don't worry if you can't concentrate on the elephant for more than 20 or 30 minutes at first. Just as taking up running or lifting heavier weights in the gym gradually builds up your strength, you can increase your powers of concentration over time. It's essential to realise that a lack of focus isn't set in stone as an immutable aspect of your personality. With perseverance and the right approach, you can continue developing your ability to concentrate, enabling you to achieve longer and deeper periods of focused work. It's crucial to understand that no one can focus 24/7. This myth needs to be debunked, because sustained focus can cause stress and is at odds with our natural attention rhythms.

Our attention comes and goes in waves, and constant focus is not only unrealistic but can also be harmful. Evolution has programmed us to scan our environment regularly for potential hazards, so our attention naturally fluctuates. Understanding and accepting these rhythms can help you develop a healthier approach to concentration. The ultimate goal is to use your attention effectively rather than constantly striving for uninterrupted focus.

BREAKFAST FOR THE BRAIN

When's the best time to schedule your elephants? Cal Newport, author of *Deep Work*, recommends doing focused work in the morning, ideally from 9am to midday, in order to make the most of your brain power.

"But I'm an evening person!" It's true that some people prefer to linger in bed and need more time to get moving, while others get up at the crack of dawn and are full of energy from the start. But make no mistake: only a minority of us are truly clear-cut morning or evening people. Most people fall somewhere in between, leaning more towards the morning type. We often tell ourselves that we're evening types: it's tempting to tack a few more hours on to the end of your day, but that means we crawl into bed too late and wake up tired. So we think: 'You see, I function much better in the evening!' Sorry to burst your bubble, but chances are you're actually a morning person with chronic sleep deprivation.

One more thing to add about staying up late, or later than you should: by staying up late, you send your body a signal that something's not right. That you need to stay awake because there's something afoot. This puts our brains into a state of wakefulness: they stay alert so they can prepare our bodies to flee or fight at any time. Staying up late raises the stress levels in your body and leads to poorer-quality sleep.

For the minority of people who do perk up in the evenings, it's not always that easy to plan their work for then. Society is simply not organised that way. Most people work from nine to five and all other activities are pretty much structured around that system. So, as an evening person, does that mean you have to attune your entire rhythm to a system that doesn't feel natural to you? No. And that's not healthy either: radically defying your own biological clock leads to long-term disruption of the circadian system. This in turn is associated with health problems such as diabetes, depression and obesity. In Chapter 3 I take a closer look at specific things you can do if your brain doesn't follow the standard biological and societal clock.

Elephants and rabbits

In my book *Better Minds* I introduced the metaphor of the elephant and the rabbits. Since then, I've mentioned it so often in lectures that I worry I'm repeating myself. And yet I've also included it in this new book, because it remains an incredibly powerful image to help us do the right tasks at the right time.

The metaphor is based on a quote from business magnate T. Boone Pickens: "When hunting elephants, don't get distracted by chasing rabbits." Unfortunately, that's what most of us do every day: we open our mailbox and whoops, we let a pack of rabbits escape. And so the first thing we do is chase after the rabbits. It feels good, because we're crossing lots of to-do's off our list. But it also takes a lot of time and energy. By afternoon we've hopefully got most of the rabbits back in their hutch, but by then we've run out of energy for hunting the elephant. And so we decide to put that big task off until tomorrow. Sound familiar? Leave the rabbits in their hutch (close your mailbox!) and tackle the elephant first.

Another tip you often hear in this context is 'eat the frog first', meaning you should tackle the most difficult task first, which is likened to swallowing a live frog. The idea behind this is that if you can accomplish the most challenging task at the start of your day, the rest of your tasks will feel easier. I'd like to qualify this slightly: an elephant isn't necessarily the most difficult or most tedious task. It's the most important task. That's a crucial difference.

Businesses, schools and other institutions also know that mornings are the best time for focus. As a manager or teacher, try to take this into account, especially if you want your staff or students to finish the most important tasks first. For example, it's better to schedule meetings and brainstorming sessions at the end of the day.

It's essential to actually block out focus time in the schedule or at least mark it clearly so the time doesn't get swallowed up by other activities. In companies that use this method, for example, you'll notice they don't schedule any meetings or get-togethers during elephant time. What's more, the office is silent then, so staff can concentrate on their duties. (In Chapter 5 I say a bit more about how you can create the right conditions for focus even in contemporary open-plan offices.)

An attention diary is a guideline, not an excuse to hide behind. Does your attention peak in the morning? Great. But of course that doesn't mean you should just muddle along or mess around the rest of the time. It's also possible to concentrate outside your natural focus time. For example, if you're excited about a particular task, feeling pressure of deadlines, oblivious to environmental factors, or simply having a highly productive day, you may even be able to sustain focus all day long. Though it's not wise to set this as a daily goal, because you'll soon overload your attention span. To focus properly, you also need to unfocus at times. More on that later.

Your attention landscape

Ever heard of the attention landscape? It's a concept I've borrowed from Florence Pérès. She says that everyone has peaks and troughs of attention, but that they create a different landscape for each of us. For example, some people notice marked differences between focused periods and lower-attention periods. Their concentration goes through peaks and troughs: they can go into hyperfocus several times a day, but they also experience several sharp dips in attention. This attention landscape could be likened to the Alps. Other people have less pronounced peaks and troughs. Their attention landscape looks more like the rolling hills of Tuscany or the Cotswolds: gentle undulations with no major differences in elevation. A third group tend to have an extended peak period every day: once they have achieved focus, they can maintain it for a long time. Their landscape is like Table Mountain: after a steep climb, it levels out to a fairly even plateau. But after that plateau their energy often runs out: having multiple focus moments a day can be exhausting.

So don't just find out when your focus peaks tend to occur – in the morning, afternoon or evening? – but also what your personal attention landscape looks like throughout the day. Armed with this knowledge, you can plan more specifically which tasks to do and when.

FIRST DO
THIS

THE THING
YOU'VE BEEN
WANTING TO DO
FOR 2,838,082
YEARS

THEN
DO
THAT!!

"HOLD ON,
NOW DO
THIS!!

BUT
DO THIS
FIRST

FIX YOUR PROCRASTINATION

Don't put off until tomorrow what you can do today. Age-old wisdom… that we collectively ignore. You know you have a crucial task to finish, but you put it on the back-burner. You tell yourself you still have more than enough time and occupy yourself with a hundred other things. Until the deadline really starts to loom and you go into full-on stress mode.

These tasks are usually not very motivating. Things like making a dentist's appointment or filing your tax return. But procrastination can also go hand in hand with fear of failure and perfectionism: it's better not to start something than realise you're not good enough.

People are often unaware of the causes of their procrastination. If you struggle time after time to get down to difficult tasks, it may be worth digging a little deeper. Maybe you're feeling overwhelmed? If so, it may help to divide up a big project – with or without the support of your manager or colleagues – into smaller, more achievable subtasks.

The question is: can we overcome procrastination? For an answer to this, American neuroscientist Andrew Huberman turned to the literature on addiction. Because procrastination does show similarities with addiction. The link between the two is dopamine.

Picture this: you need to complete a task, but you've lost your motivation. For example, all the documents you need for your tax return are spread out in front of you, but you catch yourself checking your emails every two minutes, scrolling through your social media or wandering off to the kitchen for a glass of water or a biscuit. You're procrastinating, and it's driving you crazy. In the end you decide to leave the tax return for now and get that presentation ready for work first. "Then at least I'll have done something useful. I'll sort out the tax return later."

We think we can get ourselves going by starting with something we do feel like doing. But putting things off often means they don't get done. Why? It's all in the mind: when you do something fun, a shot of dopamine gives you a high. But a high is inevitably followed by a low. Once the dopamine effect wears off, you'll feel a bit down and lethargic. So you probably still won't feel like doing that boring tax return. First you'll look for something else that does give you instant dopamine.

The solution is as simple as it is ingenious: keep on going. Just for a bit. Huberman says that if we don't linger in our lethargy but force ourselves to make a start, we can drag ourselves out of our low faster. You give yourself a little figurative push (okay, sometimes it hurts) to get going. Once you're off, the rest usually goes pretty smoothly. In other words, don't wait until you feel motivated. Start something first, then motivation usually follows by itself.

A useful tool to help overcome procrastination is forethought. Imagine it's 10am and you have an important task ahead of you but your inclination is to put it off. Try thinking ahead to tonight: you're snuggled up on the sofa with your partner, watching your favourite TV show. If you put the task off now, how will you feel tonight? Gnawed with guilt for saddling a colleague with extra work? Stressed because the unfinished task is still niggling at the back of your mind? And what if you tackle that task right now? How will you feel tonight? Relaxed, knowing it's finally been ticked off? Now look a little further ahead: how will you feel when you wake up tomorrow morning? Hassled, because the task should have been finished yesterday, so you'll have to ask for another extension? Or will you get up with a sense of pride and satisfaction because you know you persevered yesterday and made substantial progress towards your goals?

Hacking your limbic system

Procrastination can be countered by hacking your limbic system, a part of the brain that is involved in emotions and motivation. It's also the site of our internal reward system. All factors that have a lot to do with procrastination. The bottom line is that activities we avoid are often accompanied by a sense of discomfort or difficulty. Our limbic system wants to avoid this discomfort and instead seeks activities that are easier and cause less friction. Such as doing nothing.

But... by consciously exposing ourselves to unpleasant stimuli, we create a new challenge for our limbic system. If you don't like cold showers, maybe you should take a cold shower more often. This is one way to hack your limbic system and force it to deal with a new, more uncomfortable situation. It can help to break the vicious cycle of procrastination, because this 'rebooting' of your limbic system helps you get into a state of motivation and focus more easily.

GO WITH THE FLOW

Good, you've conquered your procrastination and made a start on that task. But what next? How do you get into a flow and how do you sustain it? Because there's something odd about flow: sometimes you can surf along for hours, while at other times it only takes a split-second distraction to wipe you out completely.

Maybe you remember how you felt the last time you were hyper-productive and totally absorbed in what you were doing? In a state of consciousness where you glided effortlessly through your work? In other words, when was the last time you felt in the flow? Maybe you've experienced it while riding a bike, surfing a wave, making music, singing, dancing, cooking or working on a challenging project. It won't surprise you to hear that many of humanity's most groundbreaking achievements or inventions have happened when people were in a state of flow, as pointed out by Rian Doris, co-founder and CEO at the Flow Research Collective (a renowned research and training institute focused on decoding the neuroscience behind the phenomenon of flow). Sam Altman and his team when they wrote the code for ChatGPT, Marie Curie and her revolutionary research, or Albert Einstein while developing his theory of relativity: all of it happened in a state of flow, according to Doris.

Together with his partner Stephen Kotler and thousands of professionals and organisations, Doris has spent the past few years studying how to achieve 'flow' a state of mind that allows you to be significantly more productive in your work. Doris based his research on that of another psychology powerhouse, the American-Hungarian Mihály Csíkszentmihályi, who introduced the concept of flow and wrote the seminal book *Flow: The Psychology of Optimal Experience*. It is impossible to sum up their work in a couple of pages, but I'll make an attempt. To keep things simple, I focus on the four pillars of flow: flow blockers, flow proneness, flow triggers and the flow cycle.

THREE CONDITIONS FOR FLOW

I experienced many moments of flow myself while writing this book. To be honest, even to me it's not always clear exactly what flow is. There's something mysterious about it. It's like having some kind of superpower that manifests unexpectedly from time to time. It's that moment when everything just comes naturally: your task is sufficiently challenging but not overwhelming and you feel completely in your element. Your energy levels are stable and boredom doesn't get a look-in. You float through the day on a cloud of flow and get your job done. Completely painless.

Unfortunately, the reality is often different. Our everyday lives are full of obstacles that keep us from achieving that state of flow: these are the flow blockers. One of the biggest culprits? Our precious smartphones.

Around 80% of people reach for their screens within 15 minutes of waking up. This is bad news for two reasons: not just because you fall back into the dopamine trap, but also – and crucially – because you do it first thing in the morning, which, for most people, is the best time to absorb themselves in work. Mornings are when you are most likely to get into that wonderful state called flow proneness.

Even if you ignore your smartphone, you don't automatically enter flow proneness. For that you need flow triggers. It's all about creating the right conditions that put you in a state of flow almost instantly. It was Mihály Csíkszentmihályi in the 1960s who first identified several of these triggers. Some activities are naturally rich in flow triggers, such as making music, surfing or video gaming. These activities have some features in common, which put Csíkszentmihályi on the trail of the first three flow triggers: 1) having a clear goal, 2) receiving immediate feedback, so you feel you're doing something meaningful, and 3) taking on a challenge that slightly exceeds your skill level.

Csíkszentmihályi describes flow as a state of deep engagement and satisfaction that happens when we are fully absorbed in an activity. He says we can achieve this state if we focus on three essential things:

1 *Having a clearly defined goal.* Whether you're painting a portrait, climbing a mountain or teaching your children to swim, to get into the flow you need to focus your attention on a single specific task. Multitasking and distraction are the enemies of flow. Getting into the flow requires complete dedication to one task at a time.

2 *Doing something that is meaningful to you.* A frog would rather look at a fly than a stone. After all, it can eat a fly. According to American psychologist Roy Baumeister – known for his pioneering research on self-control – we're not so very different from that frog. Our own attention and focus are also directed towards stimuli that, from an evolutionary perspective, look promising for our survival. In other words, you not only need a clear goal but that goal should also be relevant and meaningful to you. Baumeister's research also teaches us that we need to create a low-stimulus environment. Not all stimuli that trigger our evolutionary survival mechanism – think noise, extreme cold or heat, strange smells, a ringing phone – are equally useful today. So we should try to ban those from our environment if we want to get into the flow.

3 *Doing something that challenges you sufficiently.* If you want to experience flow, you need to strike a balance between challenge and skill. If a goal is too easy, we'll get bored and switch to autopilot. But if it's too difficult, we'll feel overwhelmed and become anxious. So we need to aim for goals that challenge us and test our skills, but are not completely beyond our capabilities.

Here's an example to make things clearer. Imagine you're out surfing. You spot the perfect wave and go for it. In that moment, you set yourself a clear goal that puts you in the flow: you're going to catch that wave. And yes, you do! You feel the balance on your board and the power of the waves. This provides immediate feedback that you then use to keep going: adjusting slightly here, shifting weight there. In this way you surf from wave to wave, each one a little higher and wilder than the last. A trickier wave comes along every so often, keeping you sufficiently challenged. But if a mega wave suddenly rolls in and throws you off your board, you are rudely awakened from your state of flow.

All well and good, but I suspect you didn't pick up this book because you want to improve your surfing technique. Can you also apply this theory to your work? Yes, of course: the three conditions for flow serve as a good guide in your professional life as well. Choose a clear and meaningful goal and try to eliminate unnecessary noise in advance. Challenge yourself sufficiently, but don't set the bar too high. Ideally, a task should require skills that are around 4% more difficult than your current skill level. This will put you on the right track to achieve that blissful state of flow.

Flow, the antidote to languishing

Do you sometimes feel a bit listless? You're not ill, there's nothing major going on, but the feeling you have is best described as 'meh'. In itself, there's nothing wrong with this – everyone is entitled to a dip now and then – but feeling constantly listless (for which the term 'languishing' has been coined) is a real focus killer.

Languishing is nothing new, but it gained a lot of attention during the COVID pandemic thanks to American psychologist Adam Grant. Many people at the time were feeling 'meh': they had no clear goal, felt they were generally stagnating and lacked any joy in life. And not for a few hours or a few days, but for weeks on end.

Luckily there's something we can do to fight this disagreeable feeling. Grant says that one antidote to languishing lies in embracing flow, which he describes as "that elusive state of absorption in a meaningful challenge or a momentary bond, where your sense of time, place and self melts away". He also suggests we should make more time and space for focus, and try to avoid fragmented attention, because that is the main enemy of engagement and excellence. Like Csíkszentmihályi and Doris, he recommends setting yourself enough of a challenge, but keeping it achievable. Grant says one of the clearest paths to flow is "a just-manageable difficulty: a challenge that stretches your skills and heightens your resolve".

FOCUS IS LIKE A SUNRISE

The fourth pillar of flow – the flow cycle – is often overlooked, but it's the key that leads to high productivity. Understanding how the flow cycle works can help you make major progress in terms of both productivity and job satisfaction. Eminent Harvard cardiologist Herb Benson sowed the first seed for this theory in his book *The Breakout Principle*, but it was Stephen Kotler who addressed it in more depth in his acknowledged masterpiece *The Rise of Superman*.

What does the flow cycle tell us? It reveals that the state of flow doesn't behave like an on–off switch, but works more like a dimmer. It all starts with a struggle in your body. You'll know the feeling: you embark on a task and feel your body starting to resist. Why is that? When you get to work, various hormones are released that alter the neurochemical balance in your body. This makes you feel uncomfortable, so you tend to avoid the task and seek distractions.

It's therefore important to overcome that slight discomfort you feel at the start of a flow cycle before getting into the flow. This requires a modicum of willpower but, as is often the case, practice makes perfect. In the same way that your muscles grow if you bench-press 50 reps every day, so your attention span grows if you gradually challenge yourself a little more. Specifically, if you start a task and after ten minutes feel you're getting distracted, keep on going for one more minute. The next time, keep going for five more minutes. These may seem like small, insignificant steps, but this is how you train your attention muscle. So here's a challenge: read this whole page in one go. If that works, aim for five pages and then a whole chapter. Keep adding and repeating and you'll notice that something magical happens: at some point, you let go of the struggle. Where that boundary lies is different for everyone, but as soon as you cross it, you experience genuine, sustained attention and focus.

A cycle has highs and lows. What goes up must come down. It takes a while to get into the flow, but you also can't sustain it indefinitely. Your brain needs time to recover after an intense period of focus and flow. Always working in the flow wouldn't be good for you either: when you're in the flow your prefrontal cortex deactivates to allow rapid, efficient, instinctive decision-making to occur. If you want to integrate the knowledge and skills gained in the flow, you need that prefrontal cortex again. And after the flow state comes the recovery phase, where we replenish our depleted neurochemistry and integrate the knowledge or skills acquired during flow. This isn't a switch you can flick on and off, but a gradual transition to a state of effortless, heightened productivity and creativity. This is the magic of the flow cycle – a signpost pointing to the pinnacle of human performance.

THE FIRST 90 SECONDS

If you want to get maximum output from your work, it's essential to get down to it as soon as possible after waking. Ideally within the first 90 seconds. "As soon as that?" I hear you say, "I'm still half asleep then." Yes, it does sound absurd, but scientifically this advice does stack up. When you are asleep, your brain produces a lot of theta and delta waves that are very similar to those experienced during flow. Immediately after waking, your brain is still sending out these waves, making it easy to dive straight into a hypnotic and highly focused state.

Okay, I'll admit it, hardly anyone manages to start work 90 seconds after waking. And indeed it doesn't seem socially desirable to crawl straight to your desk the minute you get up and not greet those you live with until several hours later. Let's keep it realistic: you can definitely allow yourself time to wake up. Even if you start work 90 minutes after getting up – which is a more realistic estimate for office workers – you can still get easily into a flow. But there are two key lessons to take away from the 90-second rule: an early start does mean half the job is done, and lengthy morning routines are pointless.

You see them all too often these days on Instagram and TikTok: influencers who get up two hours earlier to embark on an elaborate morning routine – a glass of hot water with lemon, an hour of yoga, then some journalling followed by a leisurely breakfast. They claim this makes them much more productive. I have to disappoint them: scientifically, it makes much more sense to keep your morning routine as short as possible and get to work as soon as you can. That doesn't mean you have to work more in a day. On the contrary, I'm also in favour of taking more breaks. Except it's better to take a first break after you've done focused work for a while, and not before.

Your brain is like a computer's memory: as the day goes on, the memory keeps getting fuller and it will become harder to get into the flow. In the morning, your brain hasn't had any other tasks to process yet. The technical term for this is low cognitive load. In plain language, it means your brain is still fresh enough to perform more complex tasks. Another good reason to schedule elephants in the morning.

Unfortunately, what do many people do in the morning, even before getting out of bed? They pick up their phones, scroll through their social media and check their emails. The result? Straight away, the rabbits escape from their hutch. Chances are you can't even enjoy a leisurely breakfast because your mind is already preoccupied with the problems of the day. On your drive to the office, the rabbits keep hopping happily around in your head, so that once you're at your computer you'll probably park your elephant and tick off the non-priority items first.

The solution? Buy an old-fashioned alarm clock and ban your smartphone from the bedroom. It can be as simple as that.

THE LIGHTER THE BETTER

Imagine you're poised at the start of a cycle challenge, set to complete it as fast as possible. The route starts at elevation, with the first 500 metres all downhill, followed by 700 metres uphill to the finish. You are ready and willing, but instead of hoisting yourself up into the saddle and streamlining your body to maximise speed and get a boost for the uphill stretch, you decide to dismount and walk down the hill while holding on to the bike (equivalent to not beginning work right away and getting off to a slow start). Not only that, but your bike is carrying some extra baggage that is weighing it down (equivalent to devouring a hearty breakfast).

As you stroll down the hill, you get distracted by birds, butterflies and supporters along the route. If you'd been on the bike, you wouldn't have noticed half of these things. You are perceiving a lot more external stimuli, precisely because you're taking it easy.

Only on reaching the foot of the hill do you decide to jump on your bike for the last 700 metres. Right away, you feel how hard the task is: every turn of the pedals is difficult, the bike seems to work against you and progress is painful. You arrive exhausted at the finish line (or the end of the working day). And tomorrow the whole process starts all over again.

What if you were to cycle downhill at full speed, with a light bike and a clear head, free from constant distraction? You'd go so fast you'd barely hear the supporters shouting, let alone be able to spot birds or butterflies. At the foot of the hill, the momentum built up would catapult you further along the ascending stretch of the route. Why not start your day like this?

Invert your morning routine

As mentioned earlier, I'm not a fan of elaborate morning routines. It's easier to focus soon after waking, so it's a waste not to make good use of those first few hours of the day. But after those initial hours of focusing, it's equally important to allow your brain some rest. So maybe you should try inverting your regular morning routine?

1 **Start with an important task.** Rather than kicking off your morning by scrolling on your phone or checking your emails, start with an important task you want to complete for the day. The elephant, in other words. This could be a creative project, a tricky job or an activity that energises you.

2 **Exercise.** Once you've finished that first task, take some time for exercise. A short workout, a bracing walk or some stretches to wake up your body and get your circulation going? Why not.

3 **Meditate.** After exercising, take time for meditation or mindfulness to quieten your mind and prepare yourself mentally for the day ahead. This can help to reduce stress and create focus.

4 **Breakfast and hydration.** Time for a healthy breakfast and proper hydration. Opt for nutritious foods and drink plenty of water to keep your energy levels up throughout the day.

5 **Plan and prepare.** After preparing yourself physically and mentally, take some time to plan and prepare for what's still to come. Write a to-do list, set priorities and organise your tasks for the rest of the day.

FOCUS ON RECOVERY

You reach the end of a flow cycle after three to four hours of work. Remember that flow isn't binary: you can't simply turn the state of flow on or off. Flow doesn't work like a light switch. It's more like a dimmer. So it's important to consciously make space to recharge after an intense period of flow. Being in the flow takes an awful lot of energy, so your brain needs time to recover before it can embark on another peak performance.

You can't perform well if you don't rest when you need to. Yin and yang: for everything you do, you need a moment where you do nothing. Unfortunately, we don't always rest as effectively as possible. I like to differentiate between passive rest and active recovery. You can lounge in front of the TV, with a beer or glass of wine in hand, or you can actively engage in the recovery process. The latter means choosing activities that help your brain to recover. Such as a short walk, an ice bath or a cold shower, or – if you prefer something warmer – a relaxing sauna.

At the office, of course, you obviously can't jump in the shower after every flow cycle. But even if you can't fit in a spot of exercise or a coffee break, you can still factor short periods of recovery into your schedule. It's important, though, to really give your brain a rest. So don't reach for your smartphone. Ideally, what you do during your breaks should be less stimulating for your brain than your work itself, especially if you are prone to procrastination. It might sound a bit strange, but staring at a blank wall for five minutes makes the task you're trying to avoid seem more appealing than the boring activity that is staring at a blank wall. (For people who work from home, this is the ideal time to empty the dishwasher or give the living room a quick vacuum, especially if you don't like doing household chores. Chances are the task you're putting off will suddenly become a lot more attractive.)

FOCUS

WORK THROUGH TO-DO LIST

CONCENTRATE FOR 2 HOURS

FOLLOW A SCHEDULE

MEET DEADLINES

STAY OFF SOCIAL MEDIA

ACHIEVE OBJECTIVES

ALSO FOCUS

GO TO BED AT A REASONABLE HOUR

GO FOR A WALK

TAKE A BREAK

MAKE TIME FOR FRIENDS

REVIEW YOUR SCHEDULE

EAT HEALTHILY

In any case, what you shouldn't do in a recovery phase is catch up on emails or check your news feed. That's far too stimulating for your brain. The problem is the dopamine-hungry 'rat' in our brain: the nucleus accumben, which has no wish to go back to the less stimulating activity you were just doing. So you keep scrolling.

Why does time go so fast?

Why does time seem to pass more quickly the older we get? There is no conclusive explanation, but there are several theories. One of these is the ratio theory: when you are four years old, one year makes up 25% of your life, whereas when you're 20 years old, one year makes up only 5% of your life. As a result, the years seem to drag when you're a child and to fly by as you get older.

Routine also plays a role in influencing our perception of time. As a child, you're seeing everything for the first time, so time seems to pass more slowly. But as you get older and find yourself in a more repetitive environment, your brain goes onto autopilot and you pay less attention to everyday events.

Another theory says that the older we get, the fewer visual images are stored in our brain, which makes it seem as if the film of our lives is playing faster. It's as if we are filming our memories at ever fewer frames per second, so the footage seems to go ever faster.

What is the link with flow? When we are in a state of flow, we are alert but not stressed. The more alert you are, the higher the 'frame rate' of your experience. When you're stressed and waiting for something or someone, time seems to stretch endlessly because you're analysing it more closely. But when you're in the flow, time actually seems to fly by: your brain concentrates on the task rather than the time.

BOREDOM REFRESHES THE BRAIN

"I'm bored." When children are at a loose end for a few minutes, the spectre of boredom starts to tap on their shoulder. Adults have often forgotten what it's like. What do you mean, bored? You've got plenty to do, haven't you? You could tidy your room, read a book, draw a picture, fold the laundry... We can always think of an activity to dispel boredom. And that is precisely the problem.

Are we still allowed to be bored nowadays? Boredom? That's just laziness. And being lazy doesn't get you anywhere. But is that right? What actually happens to us when we get bored? Or, more importantly, what happens to us if we never get bored? And what would it be like if we rid ourselves entirely of this human emotion? The answer to that last question is simple: it's not a good idea.

When we get bored, we activate a network in our brains that neuroscientist Marcus Raichle calls the default mode. It also activates when we are engaged in routine tasks that we can do on autopilot, such as folding the laundry or walking to the shop. You might think your brain is just taking a break at these times, but nothing could be further from the truth. Interestingly, this is when your brain actually gets incredibly creative.

British psychologist Sandy Mann has conducted research into boredom. She says that when we are bored the default network in our brain gets free rein and starts daydreaming. This isn't a waste of time – on the contrary. When you daydream, you cross the boundaries of conscious thought and gain access to the subconscious. That might sound a bit airy-fairy, but it's incredibly useful: in default mode, you can tie together ideas that you would never connect in an 'active' state. Archimedes' famous eureka moment in his bath? The result of a brain in default mode. An idea that suddenly springs to mind during exercise? Same thing.

When we're in default mode, we don't just come up with creative solutions to pressing problems. We also engage in what psychologists call 'autobiographical planning': we look back on our lives, take note of the big moments, create a personal narrative, set goals and figure out what steps we need to take in order to achieve them.

At least, that's what we could do, but nowadays we don't give our brains nearly enough time to go into default mode. We fill breaks at work with a spot of internet surfing. In the evenings we laze on the sofa watching a new TV series, phone within easy reach so we can quickly check on how that sports match is going. Our brains are always on, with inevitable consequences.

DELETE THAT STUPID APP

"Boredom can lead to your most brilliant ideas." That's the pitch of an inspiring TED talk by journalist, podcast host and author Manoush Zomorodi. In it, she talks openly about how boredom struck the instant she became a mother. You might think a freshly minted parent would have their hands full looking after a newborn baby but, for Manoush, the main side effect of early motherhood was a tsunami of boredom. Her whole life seemed to narrow down to pushing her baby around in a buggy, the only way to get him to sleep. She couldn't wait to get back to work. After three months, once her son had a better handle on the art of sleeping, she resumed her work as a journalist and also started a podcast. She wasted no time in buying herself the newly launched iPhone, which would make her work much easier. Or so she thought.

Zomorodi became so absorbed in her new passion that she was on the go almost 24/7. She filled every moment of downtime by responding to notifications, sending messages, checking headlines or updating her diary. She seized every spare minute to send a message to her colleagues or her husband, to show that she was busy-busy-busy. In the end, the boredom she had so despised in the first few months of motherhood became something she now sorely missed.

Through her various channels, Zomorodi launched a challenge asking people to document their phone usage. Her appeal clearly touched a nerve: countless people said they wanted to do something about their smartphone routine, but didn't know how or where to start. Zomorodi measured their average smartphone usage and came up with 60 uses a day. Some people were unwittingly spending up to 200 minutes a day on their phones. They themselves found this disturbing: it was taking up far too much time that they would rather have used for something more creative or productive.

Don't get me wrong: I'm not advocating a complete digital detox. I'm not against social media. They can be a source of relaxation and inspiration, provided they're used in a deliberate and controlled way. In my own case, I like to look at interior designs on Instagram or read interesting specialist articles on LinkedIn, but I do make sure to assign a specific block of time for this. My social media time is early on Sunday afternoon, over a cup of coffee. If you consciously schedule your time on social media, you'll be less likely to fall into the dopamine trap. And try to go for content that you find valuable and relaxing. Be selective in who you follow, as that way you'll get more enjoyment from what you see. Like so much in life, it's all about balance and awareness. If you use social media as a deliberate way to gather information, find ideas and relax, that's great.

PERFORMANCE

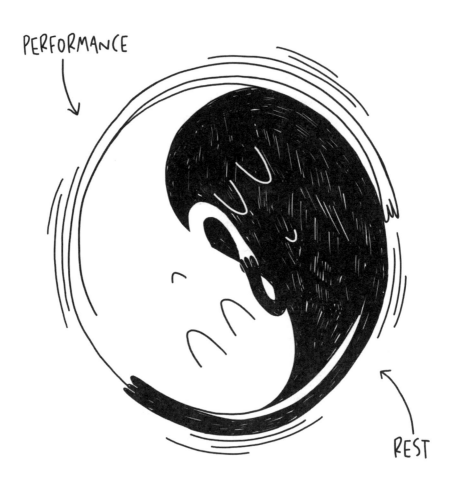

REST

A few tips from Zomorodi

1 **Delete apps that gobble hours of your time.** Addictive games like Two Dots, Tetris and Candy Crush are candy for the brain, instant dopamine shots that use clever tricks to draw you into an addictive universe of colour and earworms. Let me warn you: it can feel strange. No more notifications or updates, no more quickly completing a level or checking your likes. Anyone who deletes Facebook, Instagram, Tumblr, TikTok, Snapchat or any other app from their phone in one fell swoop may experience a feeling of loneliness or withdrawal. But what feels slightly strange or displaced at first soon turns into a sense of freedom. Blocking notifications lets *you* decide when to spend time on your social media. You take power away from your phone and regain control over your own time. Of course, this doesn't happen without a struggle. It's not like you can change or reverse that behaviour in the space of a week, or even a few weeks. But Rome wasn't built in a day either.

2 **Don't pick up your phone whenever you have downtime.** Sounds simple, but in practice it's anything but. At first it takes quite a bit of willpower not to automatically stick your hand into your pocket in search of your 'connection to the world'.

3 **Train your telephone.** A brand-new phone is like a newborn baby: everything is on and it demands constant attention. It's up to you to turn them into civilised beings and teach them how to stop screaming. So turn off alerts, push notifications and anything else designed to disrupt your concentration.

Despite our best intentions, it's not easy to ignore the constant call for attention from our smartphones. That's not entirely our own fault. As adults we're supposed to be able to control our impulses, but that's the exact opposite of what the tech developers want. Facebook, Netflix, Snapchat and their ilk do everything they can to grab and monopolise your attention. They employ thousands of engineers bent on achieving that goal. The CEO of Netflix once put it like this: "Our biggest competitors are Facebook, YouTube and sleep." Did you know that the only industries that refer to their customers as 'users' are the drug and computer industries?

The next time you reach for your phone, remember that if *you* don't decide how to use the technology, the platforms will decide for you. And ask yourself: what am I really looking for? Because if it's to check an important email, that's fine – do it and you're done. But if it's to distract yourself from hard work that requires deeper thought, take a break, stare out the window and know that by doing nothing you are actually being your most productive and creative self.

There's an app for that

If you want to change your behaviour, it first of all makes sense to analyse that behaviour. There are apps for that. (I know, feel the irony: to obtain data on your smartphone usage, you need to install an app that actually encourages usage. But sometimes needs must.)

We need to learn to deal with the constant fear of missing something or the fact of always having to be available. That's why it's smart to move the apps that constantly angle for your attention to somewhere you don't immediately see them, such as a few swipes further on your phone. You could also install an app such as Clearspace, which gives you a moment of peace before opening apps like Instagram. Clearspace asks you to breathe deeply for 15 seconds and displays an inspiring quote. Then it asks if you still want to use Instagram and, if so, for how long: 5, 10 or 15 minutes. After this time the app closes automatically, so you don't spend the whole day mindlessly scrolling.

Opal is another app that solves a common problem with iPhones and other smartphones, namely app limits. With an iPhone, you can set an app limit, but if you reach that limit it's easy to ignore it. Opal prevents that. It will block access to your apps for a given period of time and won't let you cancel or bypass. It's like locking your phone in a safe, while still having access to important apps or being able to use it in an emergency.

THE VIA NEGATIVA: THE PATH TO A BETTER LIFE

I imagine that, like most people around you, you made a list of resolutions at the start of the new year. Drink less, exercise more, waste less time on your phone, read more, watch less Netflix, spend more time with family and friends... Okay, be honest: what happened after a few weeks? Like last year and the year before, the new habits you were so excited about didn't last long.

It's pretty difficult to change our behaviour. We tend to fall back easily into old, familiar patterns. I don't have a ready-made solution, but it seems like a good idea to look at things the other way round. Instead of adding extra goals to your daily habits, it might be better to remove things that are actually hindering you or holding you back from achieving those new goals. I came across this approach, known as the *via negativa*, in a book called *Antifragile: Things that Gain from Disorder*, by Lebanese-American author Nassim Nicholas Taleb. It's similar to what Peter Hinssen calls 'yesterwork': old, outdated, inefficient practices that companies need to eliminate in order to focus on what does work.

Via negativa is a Latin phrase used in Christian theology as a way to describe God by focusing on what he is not, rather than what he is. Understanding the positive qualities of God is said to be beyond the comprehension of the limited human mind.

Here endeth the theology lesson. The via negativa approach can also be used for self-improvement. How? By focusing on what you do, not on what you don't do. Specifically, it comes down to eliminating bad habits and trying to avoid them. By stopping things that hinder you, you make room for positive change. If you eliminate negative influences, you'll discover how removing even something apparently tiny can still have a big impact.

For example, say you want to lose weight. You might choose to follow a strict diet with all sorts of rules, combined with a rigid exercise plan. Just the prospect of all these new must-dos is enough to make you not want to do it. You could also start simply and, for example, decide to stop keeping soft drinks in the house. As easy as that. It won't instantly transform you into a fitness icon, but it's a start. And once you've got some momentum, you can add more steps. Easy? Absolutely, and it also shows that avoiding the bad things can bring just as much benefit as adding in the good stuff.

Willpower works like a muscle

Changing our behaviour isn't easy. When we're under stress, our natural reflex is to fall back on what we know. In other words, our old habits. You need a lot of willpower to persevere during those difficult times, but your reserves of willpower are not infinite. So be kind to yourself: it's only human to fall back into old habits from time to time. But you should also be aware that willpower works like a muscle: the more you train it, the stronger it gets.

How to do that? American neuroscientist Andrew Huberman says that we need to look at our anterior mid-cingulate cortex (aMCC for short). Quite a mouthful for an area of the brain that acts as a kind of command centre for determination and perseverance. Just as you lift weights in the gym to strengthen your muscles, by taking on difficult tasks you stimulate your aMCC. When you challenge your willpower – for example, by not giving in to procrastination – you stimulate and strengthen your aMCC. And the stronger the aMCC becomes, the easier it will be to overcome an obstacle the next time. Interestingly, Huberman sees a link between our willpower muscle and physical exercise: exercise is thought to improve the structure and connectivity of the aMCC. So exercise keeps not only your body but also your brain healthy.

But remember that no matter how well you train the muscle, your willpower is finite. Circumstances remain a factor regardless. Imagine you're locked in a room and are only given one meal a day. You may be hungry, but you'll only eat that one meal. You don't need willpower for that. On the other hand, if you're feeling hungry in a room full of goodies, you're likely to give in to temptation sooner or later. So training your willpower is important, but it's perhaps even more important to shape the circumstances around you so that desired behaviour happens naturally. This means making smart choices about our environment and habits so we can direct our behaviour positively without constantly relying on our willpower.

JUST SIT

Exercise is good, but so too is just sitting quietly. A lot has been written in recent years about how meditation helps to find focus. It can strengthen your resilience and maybe even steer your whole life in a different, positive direction. To illustrate the effectiveness of meditation, I'd like to take you on a short journey through the history of psychology. Nowadays in the field of psychology, we are currently experiencing the 'third wave' of psychotherapy. For the first wave, we have to go back to psychoanalysis, when the theories of Sigmund Freud, Carl Gustav Jung and Jacques Lacan gained worldwide renown. Their premise was that human beings were at the mercy of various subconscious processes and that all psychological problems were deeply rooted in memory. Through intensive therapy sessions, the psychoanalysts attempted to unravel that subconscious world step by step. After that first wave, behaviourists such as Aaron Beck took over. They developed cognitive behavioural therapy, which attempted to find ways to adjust behaviour. In simple terms, a psychoanalyst explores the reasons why an alcoholic drinks, while a behaviourist looks for ways to make the alcoholic stop drinking. We are currently well into the third wave of psychotherapy, in which we are increasingly looking beyond the Western approach and borrowing from Eastern methods. Meditation is one of these.

There is a growing body of scientific research to show that meditation works. But many people are still sceptical about it. Too often, meditation is dismissed as an airy-fairy business where everyone sits around humming on mats, aiming to achieve a higher level of consciousness. That type of meditation does exist, but that image doesn't really capture the essence of meditation. There's much more to it than that. Let me start by busting some myths about meditation. No, meditation doesn't mean having to sit on some far-off mountain top and renounce all worldly pleasures. Meditation isn't difficult either: you don't need to take a long course or read any weighty tomes on the subject. And no, if you can't sit still, even that doesn't mean meditation is not for you. There are also such variations as walking and running meditation.

I can highly recommend meditating on a regular basis. You don't need to spend hours on a mat. Even a short session of just a few minutes can make a world of difference. A good exercise that brings you completely back to yourself is to focus on your breathing, in the morning just after getting up or in the evening before going to sleep, and take five very deep breaths with your full attention. I've borrowed this exercise from the mindfulness movement. Mindfulness means paying attention to the present moment. It teaches you to be aware of everything that is happening in the here and now, without wanting to change or judge it. Mindfulness is a simple technique to become more aware of what you are doing and how you feel. It helps you live more in the moment and quieten your mind. It can also help you break out of negative thought patterns and improve your ability to concentrate.

I'd qualify this by saying that meditating daily for half an hour isn't a panacea for the modern epidemic of stress and burnout. Just because you have a regular date with your meditation or yoga mat doesn't mean you can keep rushing around for the rest of the day without feeling the consequences sooner or later. That's like sticking a plaster over an open wound without treating the wound itself. Overall, you need a healthy balance between focus and unfocus time. To achieve that goal, you'll need more than just meditation.

TAKE A STEP BACK TO JUMP HIGHER

Whistling on your way to work and coming home with a bounce in your step? For a lot of people, it's something they can only dream of. Many working people nowadays suffer from chronic work stress. The causes? Often it's excessive workload, so people literally or figuratively take their work home with them. Either they stay late at work to meet that imminent deadline, or they don't manage to turn off their 'work brain' in the evening, so they're still worrying about a work-related issue. Many people also check their phones late at night or at the weekend to see if an 'important email' has arrived. In other words, we may officially work from nine to five, but our brain is in work mode 24/7. Consciously or unconsciously, we're thinking about work every minute of the day and stay 'on' all the time. That's not a healthy attitude.

In recent years, many of us have gained more freedom to plan our work. Flexible hours and working from home allow us more often to choose how and when we work. Need to leave the office an hour early because your son's running a fever and you have to collect him from school? No problem, you'll just open your laptop in the evening to answer your emails. Home and work are much more intertwined. For example, we do a quick online grocery shop within office hours and go to the dentist on our day working from home. But we also think nothing of making a work-related phone call in the evening or at the weekend if necessary.

We're lucky this is possible, as it allows us to achieve a better balance between work and home commitments. This not only gives a sense of autonomy but can also lead to greater fulfilment and satisfaction. It feels as if you can be the best version of yourself both at work and at home.

However, that flexibility can also go too far. These days we can work anytime, anywhere, so many people feel under pressure to be constantly available. They don't just open their laptops to catch up for an hour. They also answer emails while sitting on the sofa of an evening or cheering their child on from the sidelines during the Sunday football match. This can lead to high stress levels and work addiction.

The often unrealistic expectation that we should always stay connected, respond instantly to emails or even attend meetings outside of normal working hours makes it incredibly difficult to disconnect from work. We are always 'on' wherever we are, even though it's vitally important to disconnect completely from work at regular intervals. This not only reduces the risk of burnout, it also increases your energy levels, your engagement at work and your productivity. The French have a nice expression for it – *reculer pour mieux sauter*: take a step back to jump higher. If you disconnect and rest when you need to, you'll not only be happier but also perform much better. Two birds with one stone. I strongly recommend that you disconnect completely as soon as your working day is over. Why? Because consciously disconnecting every day is the ideal remedy for mental tension.

We all experience stress from time to time. Which is a good thing, as stress keeps us mentally sharp. In prehistoric times, stress helped us to act promptly on encountering a sabre-toothed tiger, whereas nowadays stress helps us to make a final sprint with full focus and get that document in on time. The main difference between then and now? Back in prehistory, stress came and went (exit sabre-toothed

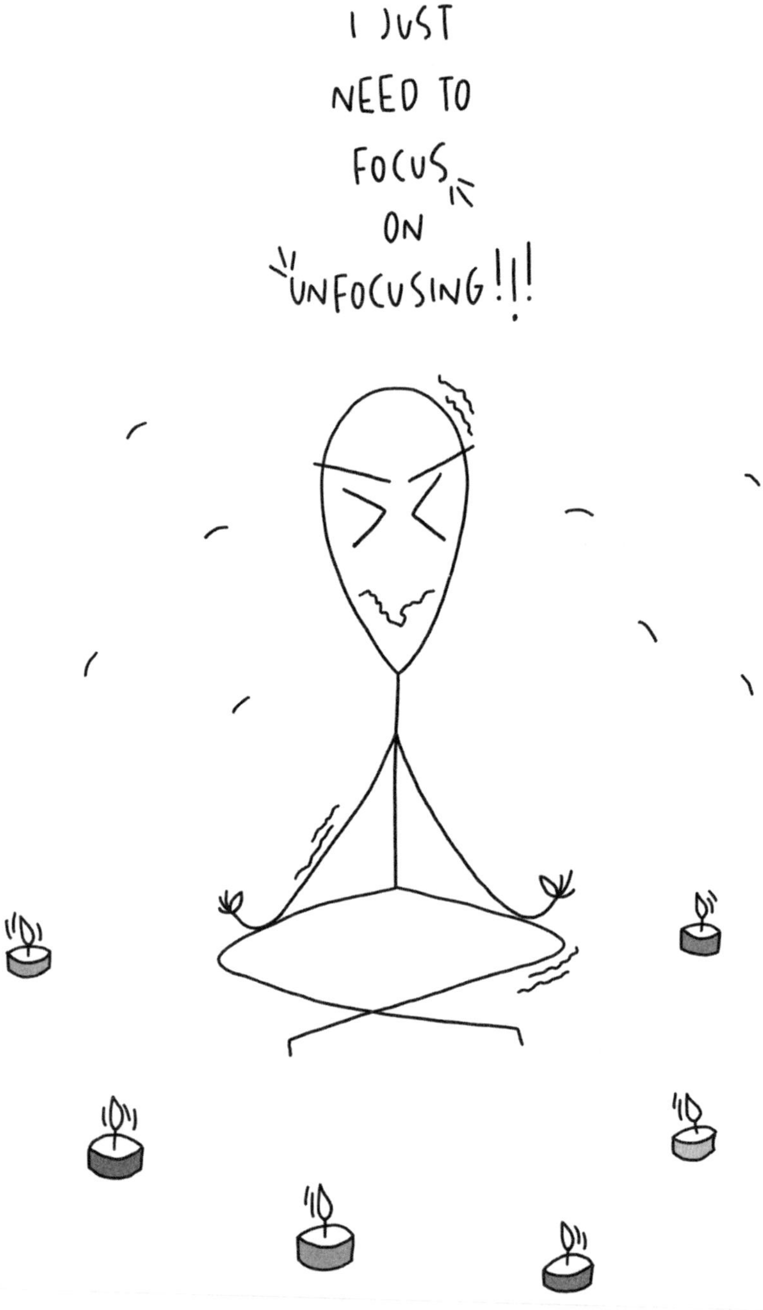
I JUST NEED TO FOCUS ON UNFOCUSING!!!

tiger, exit stress), whereas nowadays many people struggle with chronic stress. Once that document's been submitted, they still have five calls to make and ten emails to answer. The work is never quite done, it seems. From morning to evening, they spend the whole day stressed and wake up at night because their brain is urging them "not to forget to call so-and-so tomorrow".

Under chronic stress, our body and brain send out signals that we are exceeding our limits. A common symptom of chronic stress is that your thoughts and actions become noticeably more sluggish. Your work piles up, you're constantly distracted and you feel stuck in an impasse. At times like these it's hard to think creatively and making decisions becomes almost impossible. To top it all off, chronic stress often leads to a disturbed night's sleep, so you soon end up in a vicious circle. You're stressed, working less efficiently and sleeping badly, so you wake up tired, work even less efficiently and get even more stressed.

To counter this growing problem of stress, several countries around the world have introduced a 'right to disconnect'. This is a good thing, as it means you can officially be offline outside your working hours. But in fact it's just a drop in the ocean. It makes sense to disconnect after work, but even during work it's important to take microbreaks and keep your brain healthy. You can't be 'on' all the time. While taking one of these microbreaks, don't linger at your screen or reach for your smartphone or tablet. That's not a break, because you're still using your brain. Go outside, get a breath of fresh air and… give your brain the rest it needs. A quick breather, a coffee break with a colleague, a lunch break with a friend… All of these are vital opportunities to blow off some work steam and reset your brain.

An important side note: disconnecting is great, as long as you do it in the right way. Of course it's already a big plus for your brain if you don't spend the evening working on your laptop, but it's not much of an improvement if you fill that newly freed-up time with bingeing TV. Not that you can't spend a lazy evening in front of the box, but here too: everything in moderation. In the next chapter I take a closer look at the types of break that are best for your brain. But before that, I'd like to clear up a misunderstanding. Many people think they'll get their stress under control if they plan more holidays. Spoiler alert: taking a holiday is not a solution.

THE HOLIDAY TRAP

For many people, holidays are accompanied by stress. Ironically, disconnecting your batteries often means falling into a pre-holiday rut. Before you can set your out-of-office, you have a long list of to-do's to work through. Usually you don't get finished, so you're still brooding over it when your holiday begins. And maybe you've drawn up a to-do list of domestic tasks for yourself while you're on holiday: finally time to tackle the garden, deep-clean the house and fit in the compulsory visits to family. Before you know it, you'll be going from one deadline to the next while on holiday, just like you do at work.

"That won't happen to me. A holiday's a holiday! I'll go away." Not exactly a better option for that poor brain of yours, because even then you often have to organise everything. Packing bags, gathering documents and finding a pet sitter for your cat. Only to realise just before the off that there's a tear in the tent (you'd meant to repair it just after your last camping trip, but yes, you forgot...). Not until you've arrived at your destination can you really relax. Or can you?

There you are, in a deckchair on the beach on a paradise island, gazing out at infinity. But. Still. You. Just. Can't. Relax. You feel stressed and restless. The culprit? Our sympathetic nervous system, the part of our nervous system that prepares us for fight or flight in times of danger. Your heart rate accelerates, your blood pressure rises and your breathing speeds up. Other bodily functions that are currently less useful (such as digestion) are put on the back-burner. This is an excellent mechanism in acutely stressful situations (think of that sabre-toothed tiger or looming deadline), but not in times of chronic stress.

These days, our sympathetic nervous system is frequently stuck in a constant state of high alert. Our brain is overactive and the areas responsible for relaxation (the parasympathetic nervous system) get sidelined. This makes it harder and harder for you to relax. So it may well take some time to reconnect completely with your serene self while on holiday. Many people need a few days to really de-stress. Some people even tend to get ill at the start of a holiday: as the stress falls away, their bodies fall apart. Once you're well and truly relaxed and able to enjoy your holiday, it's nearly time to go home again. And right away your brain shoots into pre-work mode: "I mustn't forget to call X first. Or maybe I should finish report Y first, so Z can move on."

This is not an argument against holidays. But it *is* an argument for disconnecting regularly throughout the year so you can truly enjoy yourself while on holiday. You can't expect your brain and body to process a year's worth of accumulated stress in the space of two to three weeks. Only by taking breaks of varying lengths throughout the year can you keep your stress balance on an even keel.

If you find you can't relax on holiday, you've probably been overdoing things for too long. If so, it's sad but true to say that one holiday won't be enough for you to fully recover. Why wait for that week's holiday on the Côte d'Azur or the ski slopes before you unwind? The secret to a balanced life lies in the little breaks, the moments of relaxation you can squeeze in every day, wherever you are. These short but regular breaks are precisely what you need in order to recharge.

They help you release the stress of everyday life and face the next day's challenges with renewed energy. So why not start today by incorporating small moments of relaxation into your daily routine? A few minutes' walk, some simple breathing exercises or a cup of tea in the garden or on your balcony can do wonders for your mood and your overall well-being. Wherever you are, there is always a way to find a moment's peace and re-energise, so you can live each day with more vitality and less stress.

Fact check

I sometimes hear people say that taking a break is a total waste of time. "I haven't got time for breaks, I won't meet my deadline." Wrong! People who don't disconnect enough are cheating themselves: a task can take up to 55% longer if you don't take those much-needed breaks.

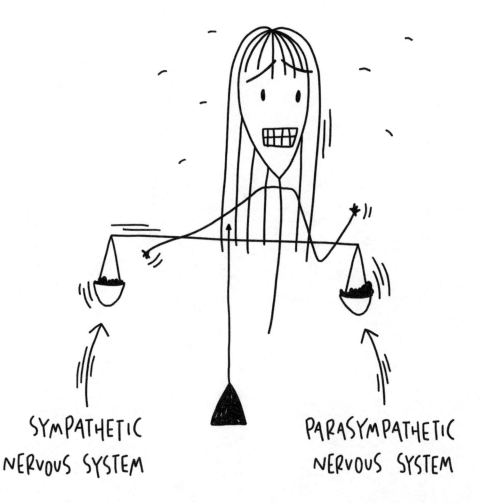

CHAPTER 3

WE ALL HAVE THE SAME BRAIN (EXCEPT WE DON'T)

From a purely scientific perspective, we all have the same brain. We are all members of one big *Homo sapiens* family and are born with brains that – if we laid them all side by side – wouldn't look very different from each other in terms of size and shape. But what individuals do with those brains is another matter. One person may have absolutely no problem focusing on a single task for hours at a stretch, while another's thoughts may fly off on a different tangent every 30 seconds.

How do we get all these different brains focused in the workplace, and is that even possible? Or should we radically rethink the way we work (and study), so that everyone with a good set of brains but a different modus operandi can reach their full potential, anytime and anywhere?

THE BRAIN IS LIKE A STACK OF BOXES

First of all, it's worth taking a closer look at how the brain works. You could compare the brain to a stack of boxes. Admittedly, this approach is slightly simplistic – the working of the brain is a highly complex area in which it's easy for the layperson to get lost – but it does illustrate the hierarchical structure of the brain:

- The bottom layer is the reptilian or primal brain, which underlies everything. The reptilian brain monitors our physical safety and is responsible for essential functions such as heart rate and body temperature. The only thing the reptilian brain is concerned with is whether the answer to the question "am I physically safe?" is "yes". If the answer is "no", it springs into action and we see the well-known fight-or-flight response.

- The second layer is the emotional part, the mammalian brain. This is where emotions come into play. Your brain continues to respond to physical threats, but emotional threats are addressed too. Am I loved? Am I wanted? Do I belong?

- The third and top layer is the neocortex, and more specifically the frontal lobe. This is the seat of our executive functions. It's the part of our brain where we think, plan and learn. This layer asks us: what can I learn from this situation?

But – and here comes the catch – when faced with physical or emotional danger, the brain switches off this top layer. This is actually normal: thousands of years ago, if you were an early human being with a lion after you, you had no time to think about how you were going to fix the roof of your hut or where you had last seen your spear. No, either you ran or you started fighting for your life. If you didn't, your number was up. In the face of danger, real or imagined, the prefrontal cortex stops working properly. That explains a lot of our behaviour. An awful lot.

NOT EVERY THOUGHT IS A CATASTROPHE

The frontal lobe could in a way be called the superhero of the brain. Under moderate stress, it's a good friend who always knows how to reassure you: "Don't worry, we'll sort this out." Our frontal lobe helps us distance ourselves from the situation, so we don't get overwhelmed by emotion and can think relatively calmly about how we're going to tackle a problem.

The frontal lobe doesn't do all that work by itself. It works closely with the hippocampus, a part of our emotional brain that has access

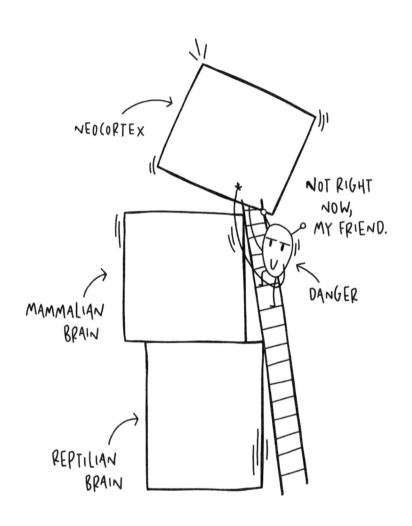

to memory. The hippocampus helps us with memories and with regulating emotions. When stress hits, the hippocampus wakes up and asks: "How did we handle this before? What strategy did we use then that we could use now?"

It's a good system, except it only works under moderate stress. Faced with what our brain perceives as acute danger, our amygdala wakes up. Where the hippocampus lays a gentle hand on the frontal lobe's shoulder with a soothing: "It'll be all right, we can fix this", the amygdala is more likely to scream: "It's all going wrong! It's the end of the world!" Who will win the battle, do you think? The amygdala, of course. "Stop trying to control your emotions. We need to focus on survival!" And instantly our fight-or-flight response is activated.

When the amygdala kicks in – like a kind of internal lion detection system – this can completely disrupt our executive functions. We're no longer thinking calmly and rationally, but acting mainly on instinct. In situations of acute danger this is pretty useful, but not every threat is a lion. Sometimes it's just an innocent cat or a curious fox. Or even just thinking about a fox. Think back to a time when you were under a lot of stress. A tough exam for example. Or that time you had to brake suddenly for a pedestrian. Chances are your heart rate has sped up and you feel tense. There's no danger, but it feels like it.

It is crucial to recognise how certain events and thoughts trigger our amygdala. Only then can we tame our inner lions and make best use of our mental strength. Otherwise, we allow our amygdala free rein and our frontal lobe will never get a look-in.

THE BRAIN'S THREE MUSKETEERS

In the frontal lobe there are three systems at work: working memory, inhibition and cognitive flexibility. When these three executive functions are working well together, we are able to retain information, suppress undesirable behaviour and switch tasks quickly. All important prerequisites for purposeful, efficient and creative brainwork.

Working memory keeps vital information constantly available, so you can keep puzzling away, piecing things together and coming up with new insights. The working memory connects the dots. But it's important not to overload the system. It's a bit like having multiple tabs open on your computer: excessive switching between tasks can cause a mental overload. Your internal computer starts to slow down, which can eventually lead to an error or shutdown. Your brain freezes and you are forced into a mental reset. Too many tasks and stimuli can lead to a mental slowdown and even a crash.

Inhibition is the strict gatekeeper who lets in only relevant information. It suppresses disruptive thoughts, habits or external stimuli that are not relevant to the task you're trying to carry out at that moment. It's a kind of filter that stops unnecessary things distracting you and helps focus your attention. In people with ADD or ADHD, an inbuilt lack of inhibition causes them to become distracted very easily. But inhibition does more than just focus your attention. It also enables you to suppress negative thoughts, which helps to reduce anxiety – a crucial part of stress management. It also improves your impulse control and memory function.

The third system in our frontal lobe is cognitive flexibility. This system is like a juggler effortlessly switching from one task to another. It is able to let go of rules and adapt quickly to new circumstances. Cognitive flexibility enables us to change perspective and find new approaches to problems.

Say you're starting a new job. It's not just your work that is changing. You also have a new journey to work, new colleagues and a new working environment. This brings many opportunities to discard old habits and develop positive new ones. But this mental flexibility is only possible if the other two executive functions are also working. This is because your primal brain finds new habits a bit stressful and will try to keep everything the way it was as far as possible. So if your inhibition isn't working properly and you lack the self-control to suppress those spontaneous reflexes – "back to what feels safe!" – you'll never achieve mental flexibility.

Only if working memory, inhibition and cognitive flexibility work well together like three musketeers will you be able to suppress old habits – as well as old thoughts and responses. You'll be able to explore different avenues of thought, think outside the box and find innovative solutions to complex problems. But if one of the three musketeers is on strike or not pulling its weight, the result can be cognitive rigidity. This feels as if you've built a wall around you that is hindering any attempt at change. You cling to old, familiar ways, even if they are no longer effective. People who are cognitively rigid become resistant when faced with new ideas or tasks. Problem-solving and creativity go out the window. "Computer says no", in the words of the satirical sketch show *Little Britain*.

Inhibition: the fragile superpower

Inhibition is incredibly important if we want to use our brain to its full potential, but it is a fragile superpower. In today's distracted world, inhibition has to kick in first thing in the morning to shut out the flood of external and internal stimuli. But actively suppressing impulses demands a lot of energy from our brain. Sooner or later, that energy runs out. The only solution? Rest and refuel.

Our inhibition not only has much more work to do than before, but we often also start at a disadvantage. When you get up feeling refreshed, your inhibition tank has been topped up. But how often do we wake up rested? As I mentioned earlier, everyone's sleep is under pressure. You've probably noticed yourself that when you're tired you can cope with a lot less and run out of patience faster. You're more prone to forgetfulness and agitation. No wonder: both your working memory and your inhibition need sufficient rest in order to function properly. So two of the three musketeers go on strike, leaving the third – your cognitive flexibility – out of action.

Stress, fear and anger have the same effect, by the way: they weaken our inhibition and thus the functioning of our prefrontal cortex.

HOW STRESS CHANGES YOUR BRAIN

Stress – especially chronic stress – causes a range of health problems, as we know. But did you know that chronic stress also has a significant impact on the brain? A brain that is constantly subjected to chronic stress begins to look different over time.

Dutch neurobiologist Brankele Frank experienced a monster of a burnout herself. She says that chronically stressed brains have been

shown to function differently from brains under normal stress. For example, people with severe burnout turn out to have smaller brains than healthy people. The grey matter shrinkage occurs mainly in the hippocampus and prefrontal cortex, two areas responsible for rational thinking, learning, memory, planning, concentration and ability to put things into perspective. At the same time, neurons in the emotional part of the brain, the amygdala, actually multiply during a burnout. This leads to hypersensitivity, irritability and emotional responses, while at the same time the ability to soothe those emotions and put them into perspective is reduced. I can already hear people who've experienced a burnout saying: "Oh dear, and now what? Will my brain stay smaller?" No, fortunately not. Through meditation, you can strengthen and even grow the grey matter at sites in the brain where it has shrunk. So you actually can 'breathe' your brain healthy again.

Johann Hari in *Stolen Focus* also talks about the impact of stress and how much it affects our brains. He cites a study by renowned evolutionary anthropologist Charles Nunne, who conducted research into insomnia. Nunne says we have trouble sleeping when we're dealing with stress and hyper-vigilance. If you don't feel safe, it takes a lot of effort to relax because your body is constantly sending signals that you need to be alert and pay attention. So not being able to sleep is not a 'failure' of your body. It is an adaptation, enabling your body to be permanently ready when faced with a major threat.

While Brankele Frank herself was sitting at home with her burnout, a couple of her friends sustained concussions. Their symptoms seemed very similar to hers: extreme sensitivity to light and sound, persistent headache, poor concentration and extreme tiredness. Research has shown that the blood of both burnout patients and people with concussion often contains higher levels of astrocyte vesicles. These are released by cells in the blood–brain barrier after a physical blow. As a result, the cells break down and excess vesicles float around in the blood. While vesicles have been found in the blood of burnout patients, they have not been found in people with depression. So burnout is actually like a kind of concussion without a physical impact.

TIME TO RECHARGE: WHY YOUR BRAIN NEEDS TO PROCESS

Human beings are not designed to operate 24/7 like a perpetual motion machine. Sometimes we'd like to be, to be constantly 'on' and glide through the day with 100% focus. On social media these days you often see life hacks popping up with tips and tricks to help you get even more out of your day. Searching for them deliberately soon takes you to a parallel world full of methods to optimise sleep or cut it to five hours a night, promising great productivity benefits. (As mentioned in the previous chapter, some people need less sleep than others, but tinkering with your sleep pattern to extract more out of your day really isn't a good idea.)

What *do* we have in common with machines? Well, we need regular maintenance too. If we don't get it, we'll break down. Certainly our mind – that part of our 'machine' that has the most input to process – needs a good reset once in a while.

In Chapter 2, I introduced the work of American neurologist and radiologist Marcus Raichle. He discovered the default mode network or DMN, now considered an essential part of our brains. The DMN is that part of the brain that becomes active when we are not consciously working on a specific task. This contrasts with the central executive network (CEN), which is engaged when we are focused on a task. This is why some researchers call the CEN the attention network: without it, it is not possible to work in a focused way.

It's one or the other: either your executive network is on and your full attention is on a task, or your default network is on and your thoughts have free rein to speculate and daydream.

When you picked up this book, maybe you hoped for some tips to strengthen your executive network. More flow, more focus, more deep work. But in an ideal world, both networks keep each other in balance. And many people nowadays have lost that balance. Do we even dare these days just to do nothing?

LET YOUR BRAIN RUN WILD

Sometimes I really enjoy letting my thoughts wander. My mind feels as free as a bird, soaring effortlessly on thermals of thought. Are we our thoughts or do our thoughts lead a life of their own? It's a question a philosopher is better placed to answer, but from a psychologist's perspective, thoughts still make excellent research material. Especially the phenomenon of spontaneous stray thoughts or 'mind wandering'.

Surprisingly, it turns out that these seemingly random rovings of the mind actually bring a wealth of benefits. It's probably happened to you too: you are deeply absorbed in a task when suddenly your thoughts start to wander. In a sense you've turned off the main route into a quieter side road where you can walk freely along the street. You start daydreaming about your next holiday or fantasising about what it would be like to be a superhero. Time seems to stand still and for a moment you are detached from reality. It's like a mini-break for your mind, and it feels great. But not only does it feel fantastic, it has real benefits for your mind. Why is that? Allowing our thoughts to roam freely creates a lot of space for creativity. So if someone tells you off for daydreaming, you can take pleasure in informing them that you may be hatching a brilliant idea.

Mind wandering can also have a positive effect on our mood. Some people think that mind wandering only pushes us towards brooding. But the opposite turns out to be true: if your mind tends to wander, it can actually improve your mood. It's like getting a mental pick-me-up, a bit like having a secret source of happiness.

But better still, mind wandering can even improve our performance at work. How so? If your thoughts wander away from what you were doing, you're distracted, aren't you? Yes, it seems that way, but it's not always the case. In fact, a little mental holiday from our work can actually help us think more clearly and make better decisions. It is as if these mental escapades are times when our mind holds a covert strategy meeting and makes plans for the future.

Yes, you've understood correctly: this book about focus is urging you primarily to unfocus more. And that means giving your mind the freedom to daydream on a regular basis. Does that sound a bit counterintuitive? That's possibly because, when you think of focus, you think mainly of what Chris Bailey calls 'hyperfocus': working on a task in focused mode. Bailey believes that 'scatterfocus' is just as important. Have you ever noticed that your best ideas tend to come to you when you're not at all focused on finding a solution? In the shower, for example. Suddenly your brain seems to tie all sorts of threads together and all at once you know how to bring that complex assignment to completion. That is the power of scatterfocus. "Letting your mind wander is different from being not-focused," says Johann Hari. I wholeheartedly agree with him there: mind wandering is an absolute prerequisite for achieving true focus.

TAKE THE RIGHT BREAK

Working hard but just can't get through that report? Can't make heads or tails of a task you could knock off in five minutes at another time? Feeling suddenly overwhelmed by everything on your plate or stuck in a cycle of negative thoughts? If any of this sounds familiar, you urgently need a mental reset.

We can reboot our brains just like we do with a computer. But is it just as easy? Pretty much. We don't have an on–off switch, but we can definitely get our brain out of sleep mode so we can get back to focused work.

We can do this by taking the right break. A short break can help your brain to process information and recharge. What exactly should you do in that break? Various things, as long as they allow you to refuel both mentally and physically.

A good tip is to decide in advance how long you want to work before taking a break. It helps to set a timer so you stick to your intended break time. In this way, you can balance the length of your breaks with the time you spend working. By deciding in advance how long you're going to work, you create a sense of urgency and focus, which helps you achieve your goals.

A good break is one where you don't take in any new information and consciously allow your thoughts to wander. Breaks where you do nothing are the most effective, because stimuli are minimised and it's easier to return to work without distraction. By letting your thoughts run wild during your break, you give your mind a chance to rest and recharge so you can feel refreshed and focused when you go back to work.

What you shouldn't do during a break is watch TV, check social media or play video games. These can disrupt the focus you've built up. Instead, choose activities that nourish your body and mind, such as going for a walk, having a healthy snack or taking a nap. By consciously choosing activities that energise you and enhance your concentration, you can more effectively recharge and prepare yourself for the next work session.

The key to the best break!

- **Plan well.** So what can you do during your break, long weekend or holiday? People who set personal goals during their leisure time – such as learning new skills, meeting people or pursuing a hobby – report being happier with their lives. This is because setting goals helps us to recharge and use our time efficiently. A tiny "yes, but" is in order here: don't see your goals as a to-do list, as this can take the fun out of pursuing them and make them feel like work.

- **Exercise, ideally outdoors.** This is surprisingly more effective than passive 'rest and relaxation', such as watching TV or scrolling through social media. Studies have shown that regular exercise during breaks – even a short two-minute walk – boosts energy levels, improves productivity and promotes creativity. So go for a walk around the block near your office. Park your car a five-minute walk away and don't check your mails en route. Fetch a coffee from the coffee bar around the corner instead of using the drinks machine at work.

- **Change your environment.** A change of surroundings allows you to disconnect from your everyday life. You don't always have to go far to enjoy yourself: a small change of scene sometimes works wonders. Whether it's an island in the Caribbean or that pretty park ten minutes from home, you're in a whole other world, both physically and mentally.

- **Going on a trip?** Why not leave your digital devices at home? Or take them with you in case of emergency, but put them in the hotel safe. Spend your daily screen time on that book you never find time for, play games with your kids, do sudokus or crossword puzzles. Or stare at the sea, the trees or the birds wheeling overhead. A true moment of rest makes us feel more connected to those around us and stimulates our creativity.
- **Screen guilt?** It's not always possible to unplug completely and leave your smartphone, tablet or laptop untouched for three weeks, which may leave you feeling guilty. If this is the case, use your screen time wisely. Doom-scrolling on social media doesn't give your brain and body the rest they need. Before you know it, you've been scrolling for an hour, and browsing a second-hand auction site has led to a celebrity's home tour, sparking a quest for their trendy decor item and a shout-out to your Instagram followers to help you find it. Best avoided. But if you *are* online, ask your friends to support you in your physical challenge by lending inspiration for fun things to do or challenging your brain with puzzle games. Wordfeud? On you go!

NOT EVERY BRAIN WORKS IN THE SAME WAY

We all have the same brain, but not every brain works in exactly the same way. If we want to engage everyone in the workplace – and in everyday life – and create an inclusive environment, it's important to embrace individuality while also considering the needs of people whose brains work differently. That differentness needn't put a brake on a company's success for example, but can actually promote it. Especially if we can allow people with neurodivergent brains to shine in their full uniqueness. It's important to make sure that everyone is in the right place where they can flourish best and tap into the full capacity and potential of their brains.

Neurotypical versus neurodivergent

Neurotypical and neurodivergent describe different ways in which the brain can work:

- **Neurotypical** means that someone's brain functions in a way that is considered 'normal' or average in society. People who are neurotypical don't usually experience neurological or developmental disorders. They follow the standard developmental and behavioural profile common to most people. For example, a neurotypical child usually learns to talk and read in line with expected developmental milestones.
- **Neurodivergent** means that someone's brain works differently from the average or 'typical' pattern. People who are neurodivergent have unique neurological traits that can lead to differences in thinking, learning and behaviour. For example, a child with autism may have difficulties with social interaction and communication that set them apart from neurotypical children. A person with dyslexia may experience challenges in reading and writing, but may also have exceptional skills in other areas, such as problem-solving or creativity.

The unfortunate reality in society is that there is often a stigma attached to neurodivergent conditions such as ADHD and other neurodivergent traits. And society is principally structured according to a traditional nine-to-five work schedule, although many people with a neurodivergent brain find that their most productive times often fall outside standard office hours. And modern-day offices are often ill-suited to people who find it difficult to concentrate in a large, open space (more on this in Chapter 5).

As a result, people feel ill at ease in the workplace and drop out. This is doubly unfortunate: not only are they unable to reach their full potential, but companies also lose incredibly valuable members of staff. It is therefore crucial to show more understanding and flexibility in the way we organise work. More attention and space for diversity in work styles and schedules would not only benefit people with neurodiverse brains but also enrich society as a whole with a wider range of talents and perspectives.

IS EVERYONE NEURODIVERGENT?

Doctors and psychiatrists have traditionally used a tool called the DSM to determine whether or not someone is neurodivergent. The Diagnostic and Statistical Manual of Mental Disorders (DSM, now in its 5th edition) lays down certain criteria for neurodiverse conditions. If you meet a given number of those criteria, you get a diagnosis. If you don't tick the necessary boxes for, say, ADHD, then you don't have it.

But just as a rainbow has more than seven colours – green doesn't instantly become yellow – there are many nuances when it comes to neurodivergence. Being neurodivergent is not a simple matter of yes or no. It's a complex spectrum. Some people are not on the spectrum at all, while others are on it to a greater or lesser extent. You could compare it to a colour palette where each individual represents a unique blend of colours.

In the case of ADHD symptoms, there are eighteen criteria divided into two main categories: nine for inattention and nine for hyperactivity/impulsivity. Some people meet seven of them, others three. And still others tick off boxes on the checklists for both ADHD and autism. Neurodivergence comes in varying degrees. It's important for individuals to check for themselves the extent to which traits apply in their own case. I don't mean you should set out to pin a label on yourself, but it may help to know whether some of your own traits match those of a neurodivergent brain.

Within this spectrum, people can have different abilities in terms of concentration and stimulus processing. Some people thrive in complete silence, while others do better in an environment with some background noise. But even within these categories, there is variation. It is not just a question of whether or not you need silence, but also important to identify the specific conditions that work best for you. Maybe earplugs are a lifesaver for you in a noisy environment, or maybe you find peace and calm at home in a setting with only a few people around you. And that's by no means the whole story: in an office environment you also often have other stimuli to contend with. For instance, some people with autism will adopt a slightly odd physical posture in order to focus. Many people with ADHD can only focus by 'body doubling', having another person beside them as a supportive presence to add motivation.

Although there are general guidelines and tools available that many people find useful, it's essential to understand your own needs and preferences. This means not only identifying what works for you, but also adapting and refining those tools to suit your unique way of functioning. It's about finding a personal harmony between who you are and how you operate best in different circumstances.

A LOOK AT ADHD AND AUTISM

An interesting voice when it comes to neurodiversity is that of Belgian copywriter Magali De Reu. In a fascinating book about her own autism and ADHD, she explains how she tries to arrange her life to match the world around her, a world that is – let's be honest – geared mainly to more neurotypical brains. She also busts some stubborn myths and clichés about focus in neurodivergent people. And yes, we all know them, and they're sometimes absurd:

> 'If something really matters to you, you _will_ do it.'
> 'Adding or strengthening a reward element will help.'
> 'Stricter consequences give you more willpower to focus.'

These statements don't hold true for people with a neurodivergent brain, because their motivation system works a bit differently.

As a general rule, many people with autism often thrive in a structured, calm, low-stimulus environment, though that's only one of the many manifestations of autism. Predictability, routine and clear instructions help them to feel safe and grounded. Intrinsic motivation, such as interest in a topic or task, is often more powerful than rewards or other external factors such as deadlines or social expectations. They can become deeply focused and get into the flow when engaged in activities that match their specific interests or passions. Such activities can range from obsessive study of a particular subject to following meticulous routines.

The fact that people with autism can become deeply focused when engaged in a task that matches their passions and interests is fairly well-known. But people with ADHD can go into hyperfocus too, albeit with some differences. In terms of duration and consistency, hyperfocus in autism is often prolonged and consistent, and

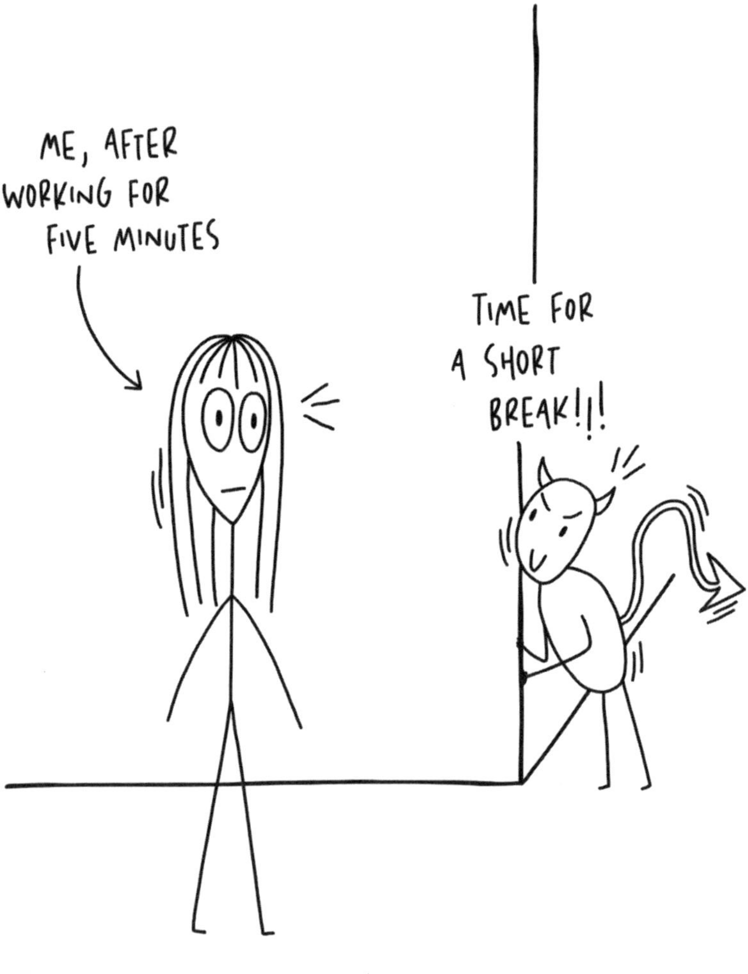
ME, AFTER
WORKING FOR
FIVE MINUTES
TIME FOR
A SHORT
BREAK!!!

reserved for specific fields of interest, whereas hyperfocus in ADHD fluctuates more and depends on the stimulus value of the task. The triggers are different too: hyperfocus in autism is usually triggered by deep, intrinsic interests, whereas hyperfocus in ADHD is mainly driven by external stimulation and rewards. And in terms of functionality, hyperfocus can have both positive and negative effects in both cases, but the regulation and consistency of this focus differ between autism and ADHD.

ADHD or attention deficit hyperactivity disorder. The official term suggests a lack of attention. This is misleading: a person with ADHD doesn't have too little attention, but too much. Someone with a neurotypical brain can differentiate between primary and secondary issues fairly easily under normal circumstances. Someone with ADHD sees every stimulus as equally relevant, so they want to focus on far too many things at once. This can make it hard to get into a flow. But once they cross that threshold, they can be extremely focused and productive, especially when engaged in tasks that both interest and challenge them. So intrinsic motivation is very important for people with ADHD as well. At the same time, extrinsic factors – such as clear deadlines and a healthy atmosphere of competition – can also be positive for their focus, as they offer an immediate reward and create a sense of urgency.

White, pink or brown?

Coping with a plethora of external stimuli is often challenging for both people with ADHD and those with autism. Magali says it is anything but easy for her to focus when there is too much ambient noise. In this situation she often puts on headphones playing a mixture of white and brown noise. The headphones act as a kind of auditory block that muffles background noise and improves her focus.

You've probably heard of white noise. The murmur of the sea, the gentle hum of an extractor fan, a babbling mountain stream... This kind of constant noise contains every audible frequency at equal intensity and helps to mask distracting background sounds, making it easier to concentrate on the task at hand.

But there are also options such as pink and brown noise. Pink noise is a bit like white noise but sounds softer and quieter, like the pattering of a rain shower or the rustle of wind in the trees. If you want to read a book in a busy café, for example, pink noise can help soften the din and create a calm atmosphere. Pink noise not only improves your focus but can also enhance your quality of sleep. And sleeping better means being sharper and more focused during the day. Fancy falling asleep to the soothing sound of rain tapping against the window? Yes please!

And what about brown noise? This is the deep roar of a waterfall or the rumble of distant thunder. Brown noise lowers the higher-frequency sounds of pink noise and is more of a deep hum. If you want to meditate or simply relax after a long day, brown noise can have a grounding and calming effect, perfect for reducing stress and anxiety. For someone with ADHD, brown noise can help calm the mind and improve focus. But even if you don't have a label, it may be worth finding out what brown noise can do for you. After all, every brain is different, and you never know what you'll respond well to.

URGENT IS NOT THE SAME AS IMPORTANT

People with ADHD and autism often confuse importance with urgency because they have a distorted sense of time:

- *Important tasks* have a long-term impact and bring us closer to long-term goals. Examples include working on a big project, developing a new skill or building strong relationships. These tasks or projects often have no immediate deadline but are crucial for long-term growth and success.
- *Urgent tasks* often crop up unexpectedly and feel like they need to be tackled immediately, regardless of their long-term impact. Examples include finishing off a project before a looming deadline, answering an urgent query from your boss or fixing something that has just broken down.

For people with a neurotypical brain, the difference between the two is clear: a huge project that needs to be finished in 40 days is important, and a task that needs to be finished within half an hour is urgent.

To people with ADHD, an urgent task often feels important. Because they often have lower levels of dopamine in their brains, they are more susceptible to things that bring an immediate reward. So they often prioritise the now over the future. Urgent tasks rise to the top of their to-do list and displace the things that are actually important. When something is urgent, it demands immediate attention. The feeling of 'I-need-to-do-this-now-or-it'll-be-too-late' masks the fact that things that attract attention are probably not all that important (and may even take us further away from our long-term goals). ADHD brains get carried away in the grip of last-minute panic, possibly due to their greater need for immediate rewards. In other words, their brains are even more likely than neurotypical ones to be distracted by the proverbial rabbits they encounter, leaving them with hardly any time or energy for elephant hunting.

AUDHD

If there is one thing Magali has taught me, it's that there is no one-size-fits-all solution. ADHD and autism produce a complex dynamic, especially when they occur in combination. People who have both autism and ADHD – which Magali De Reu calls AuDHD – often have a unique combination of challenges and strengths. Indeed, it can sometimes seem as if the symptoms of the two conditions are contradictory. For example, people with autism often benefit from predictability and structured environments, whereas someone with ADHD may desire challenge and variety. In someone with AuDHD, this can create an inner struggle between the need for routine and the urge for variety. Or, as Magali so beautifully puts it: "Sometimes I feel like a walking contradiction."

It is not easy to assess which condition has the stronger effect, because people with autism and ADHD may show different symptoms, and the severity can vary from person to person. And you are always much more than your ADHD and/or your autism: your individual character traits and the context in which you live and work also play an incredibly important role. So it's vital to find what works for you. Magali and I can offer you certain tools from a neuropsychology perspective, but it remains a matter of trial and error. So think of the following tips like a menu. You don't necessarily have to eat every dish. (But you can of course, if you're really hungry.)

FACTOR IN PLENTY OF
REWARDS ALONG THE WAY

Dopamine plays an important role in motivation and focus. People with ADHD have less dopamine in their brains, which makes it harder for them to complete tasks that don't offer immediate rewards. This explains why they often find it very difficult to set and pursue long-term goals. People with autism may also experience dopamine-related problems, but there is no conclusive research on this as yet.

Does this mean that focus is impossible for an ADHD brain? Not at all. Sufficient dopamine in your brain boosts your motivation because it activates your reward system. If you naturally produce too little dopamine, you can bypass the system by giving yourself enough rewards along the way. How? By breaking down the long-term goal into smaller, manageable steps. Or by using visual aids that help to focus and maintain your attention. Here are a few specific examples:

1 *Use time-blocking and visual planners.* Time-blocking, where you assign specific tasks to certain time slots in the day, can help to create structure and reduce distractions. A good example is the Pomodoro technique: in this popular time management method, tasks are split into short intervals of focused work, followed by short breaks. This can help to maintain focus and heighten productivity. Visual planners, such as whiteboards or apps using colour codes, can help you organise tasks more visually and prioritise better.

2   *Set up reward systems.* Don't focus solely on the end result, but reward yourself along the way. Rewards can range from a small treat (such as a quick break or a snack if you've worked solidly for a few hours) to bigger items (such as a day out or a personal indulgence if you've met a key interim goal).
3   *Bring in external support.* A coach, mentor or therapist may be able to help you set goals, develop custom-made strategies and provide necessary guidance and encouragement.
4   *Get enough exercise.* Regular exercise can help reduce hyperactivity and impulsivity, and improve your concentration and overall mood. Activities such as walking, cycling or yoga can have positive effects on the well-being of people with ADHD.

Do you have a team member with ADHD? If you do, keep the above tips in mind. Many companies don't reward until the finish line. Wouldn't it be nice to get a few more pats on the back along the way? This doesn't only apply to people with ADHD, by the way. It's nice for any employee to receive regular direct feedback, whether or not it's linked to a reward. So don't withhold feedback until a major project is completed; make sure you consult and communicate along the way.

MAKE FOCUS A VERB

When you get bogged down in work, it is easy for you to get stuck and for progress to stall. But in just ten minutes you can make a world of difference. Is there a trick for that? Yes, there is! For example, you can reformulate your tasks using active verbs. This makes tasks instantly clearer and easier to tackle. Examples are 'send email to colleague', 'do the dishes' or 'pay bills'.

I go a step further. Take 'pay bills', for example. This may sound like a monolithic task, but if you break it down into individual steps it becomes much more manageable:

1 Collect together all unpaid bills.
2 Log in to your banking app or website.
3 Enter the payment details.
4 Make the payments.

Dividing tasks into smaller chunks not only makes it easier to get started, but also allows you to be much more focused. Instead of feeling overwhelmed by thoughts such as "I urgently need to sort out my paperwork", you opt for clear, achievable steps that you can tackle immediately.

FOCUS ON TIME RATHER THAN RESULTS

If you have ADHD it can be difficult to estimate time accurately, which can lead to frustration and demotivation. Here too, some clever hacks come in handy. Instead of setting results-based goals, such as 'I'm going to write this text today', you can choose to set time-based goals, such as 'I'm going to work on this text for an hour today'. Other examples are:

'I'm going to work on that report twice, for half an hour each time.'
'I'm going to clean for 20 minutes.'
'I'm going to work on my invoicing until 1pm.'

When working on the task, use a time log to keep track of how long it takes. By doing this, you'll get better at estimating how much time a task will take you in future.

A CHANGE OF TOOL CAN HELP

If you notice your attention starting to wane during routine tasks, you can decide to approach them in a new and exciting way. For example, if your job involves creating designs, instead of using your usual software you could challenge yourself by trying out a new graphic design program. Blending familiarity with a touch of novelty gives your task a fresh dynamic, enhancing your engagement and focus. It's a good way to bring more variety into your work and boost your creativity and motivation.

FROM TO-DO TO TA-DA!

A 'ta-da!' list, according to Magali, can be a powerful tool to motivate yourself and gain a sense of achievement, especially on days when progress is hard-won. It differs from a traditional to-do list in that, instead of just adding new tasks, you also take time to acknowledge what you've already achieved. This can help you see your progress and give you a sense of accomplishment, even if you haven't achieved all the big goals yet.

The idea is to focus not only on what remains to be done, but also on what you have already achieved. By doing this, you can encourage yourself and remind yourself that you *are* making progress, even if it sometimes doesn't feel like it.

The items on a 'ta-da!' list can range from simple everyday tasks to more substantial achievements. Too often we focus mainly on the bigger to-do's and lose track of smaller tasks. For example, watering plants, walking the dog or putting the bins out on time are all small tasks that are easy to overlook. But these are important and can be satisfying to complete. Answering emails promptly or calling a client are work-related tasks that can go on your 'ta-da!' list.

Writing down and acknowledging all these achievements will make you feel fulfilled and even proud. It can also help motivate you to keep going and complete the rest of your tasks. The key thing to remember is that progress is not always linear, and that even small steps in the right direction are important. Of course, let's not forget that you still need to keep finishing off those elephants. The aim is not to draw up a never-ending list of small tasks that can be quickly ticked off. So make sure you get the balance right and don't just hunt rabbits. One way to keep working on an elephant without feeling overwhelmed is to put smaller interim steps and goals on your 'ta-da!' list.

FORGET THE FROG, EAT THE CANDY

Instead of focusing on the hardest task of the day and finishing it first ('eating the frog'), try starting with the tasks you enjoy most, the ones that energise you. Especially for neurodivergent people, this approach can be valuable as it allows them to capitalise on their strengths and positive experiences. They maintain a positive mindset and build motivation for the rest of the tasks on the list.

Magali says she often goes about it like this: to get herself into a productive flow, she starts with tasks that she can finish quickly and that give instant gratification. This gives a positive impetus that boosts her motivation and productivity. Seeing immediate rewards for your efforts is a powerful way to stay motivated and build momentum for the rest of the day. Feeling that satisfaction also brings a sense of achievement, which in turn boosts your energy and focus.

However, it's important to decide in advance how much candy you're going to eat. Or chances are you'll only tick off the fun or easy tasks. For people with a neurotypical brain, I still recommend tackling your elephant of the day as soon as possible, but for people with ADHD, starting with a snack can give that extra dopamine shot you need to take on a longer task with complete focus.

All aboard

In my honest opinion, the prevailing culture in the business and professional world is still such that the experiences of people with different working styles and neurodiversities are overlooked. Unfortunately, we also find these shortcomings on platforms such as LinkedIn. There is still a great deal of work to be done when it comes to inclusiveness and diversity. It is not enough simply to run a diversity, equality and inclusiveness (DEI) campaign if there are deep-seated problems in an organisation. Resolving these calls for a more radical change in mindset and culture. We need to recognise that there are different working styles and outlooks, and that this diversity can be a source of strength and innovation. It is time to take action. We need to strive for a business world where everyone has equal opportunities and recognition, regardless of background or neurodiversity. We need to work together to create an environment where everyone's voice is heard and valued, and where diversity is embraced as a source of strength and growth.

CHAPTER 4

THE MYTH OF THE MULTITASKING BRAIN

I can work on different assignments or projects at the same time. Mornings start with replying to emails while answering students' questions in a WhatsApp group, while a podcast on Hegelian philosophy plays in the background. And there's a document open on my laptop that I'm adding ideas to while a loaf of bread bakes in the oven.

You might be thinking: how productive! Nothing could be further from the truth. Two important emails have gone unanswered this morning. But they *have* been marked as read, so chances are I'll never look at them again. My students can move on with their work, but I'll need to listen to that podcast again. Meanwhile my publisher is pressing me, as the document on my laptop is still no more than a draft, and the bread has come out of the oven a tad on the burned side.

As I've said many times before, multitasking is a myth. We can't perform two tasks simultaneously if both of them require cognitive effort. I can't do it, you can't do it, busy 'supermoms' can't do it. No one can. Why not? Because our brains simply don't work that way. We think our brain can 'fragment' itself and do each job equally well, but that's not the case. Multitasking is counterproductive: we delude ourselves that we'll get more done, but at the end of the day we have done less and the quality in particular has suffered.

SWITCHTASKING

Multitasking? It's a trap we all fall into, often without realising it. Why are we so susceptible to the idea? Because our brain wants to avoid boredom like the plague. Multitasking is a reliable way to make sure you have enough variety. And you often get patted on the back for it too. How many times have you seen job ads that say: "Must be an excellent multitasker"? And the modern world – where many of us spend most of the day at a screen – forces our brains to keep constantly jumping from one task to another.

An example? Suppose you decide to focus on a single task: making dinner. That seems pretty simple, but from the instant you decide what to make – lasagne! – your cognitive control network kicks in. This includes areas of your brain that are involved in planning and executing goal-focused behaviour. Such as writing a shopping list, estimating prep time and visualising the end result. At times like these your brain combines external information, such as the ingredients in your fridge, with internal information, such as your recall of your grandmother's recipe. The areas of your brain involved in decision-making and planning work together to create a mental model of the cooking process. This enables you to think through step by step which ingredients you need, what order to use them in and how long to cook them for.

So a seemingly simple task demands quite a lot from your brain. American psychologist Gloria Mark compares this process to a kind of mental whiteboard that you gradually fill up with writing. If you've made lasagne many times before, all you need are a few keywords. If this is your first time at the stove, it probably won't be enough to scribble a few ingredients on your whiteboard. Better to write down step by step what to do and when.

And what if you get distracted while cooking? Say your smartphone lights up. Or you get a call from a good friend. In a flash, your brain switches to a totally different task: I'll just pick up, maybe it's urgent. And hot on its heels comes another switch: maybe just turn that ring down a touch, or the veggies will burn. This switching between tasks can go pretty smoothly if you're making lasagne for the hundredth time and you're just having a relaxed chat with your friend. But if you're not a confident home cook and your friend on the other end of the line needs a deep, empathetic conversation, it'll be a very different story. Both tasks will demand full attention. Your brain will have to switch constantly between two information sources and is bound to make mistakes. Chances are you'll cut your finger or your friend will feel you're not fully there for them.

We often think we're doing two things at once, but actually we're splitting our attention between two or more separate tasks and our brain is constantly switching from one task to another. So we're not multitasking but 'switchtasking'. Only if you can operate fully on autopilot can you do two things at once – like catching up with that friend from earlier during a stroll in the park.

YOUR RACING DRIVER BRAIN

Now you're probably wondering: why *shouldn't* I switch from one task to another? Variety is the spice of life, isn't it? When lecturing I often hear people say: "Doing lots of things at once keeps my brain sharp." I have to disappoint these people too: constantly switching between two or more tasks isn't good for your brain. It is like standing at a huge buffet table, heaping your plate with all kinds of random things, but never really taking the time to enjoy any one dish.

You may be under the impression that switchtasking helps you get a lot done, but you're actually putting unnecessary pressure on your brain. According to US-Canadian cognitive psychologist Daniel Levitin, every time we shift our attention from one task to another our brain has to flip a neurochemical switch. That takes energy, and lots of it. When we're 'multitasking', we're actually shifting from gear to gear like a Formula 1 driver hell-bent on victory, and using a huge amount of energy. No wonder we're often so tired at the end of the day.

Especially in today's distracted world, our brain is constantly racing. Gloria Mark found, for example, that office workers are able to

work on a task for around three minutes before being distracted or switching to another activity. Yes, you read that right: three minutes. Mark also says that we check our email on average 74 times a day and switch tasks on the computer up to 566 times a day.

You might think that a temporary distraction isn't so bad. That doing something else for a while doesn't immediately break your focus, so you can just carry on with your work. Again, I have to disappoint you. American neuroscientist Michael Posner is an authority when it comes to research into attention and concentration. In one study, he investigated how long it takes to return to a state of focus after being distracted. It takes much longer than you think: Posner's research suggests that when people are distracted during a task it takes them an average of 23 minutes to regain the same deep concentration as before the interruption.

Let that sink in: it takes 23 minutes to get back to full focus, but we are distracted every three minutes on average. No need to draw you a picture, we are stuck in a vicious circle. And no small one either.

THE SWITCH COST EFFECT

If you hooked people up to a brain scanner for a week, you'd see that their brains almost never get a rest – they just keep on going like a perpetual motion machine. At home and at work, we are constantly on and distraction lurks around every corner: a quick check on your phone, emailing on the go, a colleague dropping by for a chat, the printer crashing, an app reminding you to read that email... We are constantly switching from one task to another. And we pay a price for that. Neuroscientists talk about the switch cost effect: the extra time and mental energy needed when transitioning from one task to another. Every time you switch activity, your brain has to adapt to new information, goals and contexts. And that switch comes at a cost: we make mistakes, work less efficiently and sacrifice productivity.

A telling example of the switch cost effect is checking emails while working on a project. This situation probably sounds familiar: while absorbed in a creative task, you get an email alert. Do you decide to look at the email right away or do you put it off? In the second scenario you are distracted for an instant but can probably pick up the thread relatively quickly. In the first scenario, you completely disconnect your initial activity: you read the email, find the necessary info, formulate an appropriate response, send it, and then have to dive back into your report. Where were you again? You first have to find the proverbial thread before you can pick it up and get back to full focus.

When you constantly switch tasks, not only do you need more time and/or make more mistakes, it also makes you physically tired. Constant task switching is like a sports competition where your brain continuously races from one discipline to another, having to apply different skills each time. Continuous switching – remember Levitin's neurochemical switch – depletes certain chemicals in your brain. Such as noradrenaline, which makes us alert and energetic. But also acetylcholine, which helps us to concentrate, and dopamine, which helps us to finish tasks. The dangerous thing is that we usually don't even realise it, because when we switch from one task to another we actually get rewarded with a shot of dopamine. In a nutshell, switchtasking makes us feel good in the short term but exacts a price in the long term.

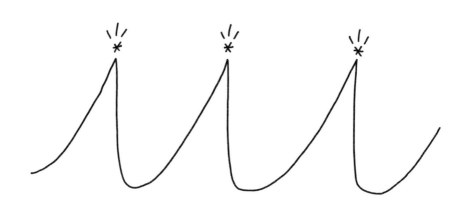

POPCORN BRAIN

Picture the scenario: right in the middle of an important presentation, you suddenly realise you forgot to feed your cat this morning. You want to fix this asap, so you reach for your phone and message your housemate. But just then a notification pops up: your favourite cosmetics are on sale. It's a tempting offer, so you take a quick peek. Before you know it, you've added six products to your shopping cart, listened to the techno version of Taylor Swift's *Wildest Dreams* in your head four times and booked a cinema ticket for later in the week. When you finally focus back on the presentation, the meeting is over and you've forgotten all about your hungry cat. This, dear reader, is a classic case of a popcorn brain.

'Popcorn brain' describes those moments when your thoughts and attention shoot off in all directions due to digital distraction. It is as if your brain warms up and starts 'popping' due to the constant stimuli of notifications and online temptations. This term, coined by American researcher David Levy, illustrates how modern technology can undermine our focus and productivity.

I first came across the popcorn brain in the popular podcast *Diary Of A CEO*, when Dr Aditi Nerurkar said she believes almost everyone suffers from this condition sooner or later. How right she is. Think about it: what do you do while waiting for a train? Exactly, you're on your phone. And while waiting for your coffee? When you're the first to arrive at a restaurant and are waiting for your friends? On the toilet? Check, check, check! I bet you have a popcorn brain too. No need to panic: popcorn brain isn't the same as internet addiction. Internet addiction turns your life upside down, but a popcorn brain is simply part and parcel of modern life.

What is interesting about the popcorn brain is that it has a link to prehistoric times, back when we still roamed the savannah and sheltered in caves. When night fell, there was always someone keeping an eye out. The tribe slept while the night watchman scanned the vicinity for danger. Nowadays, all of us are the night watchman. The reason we are constantly scrolling on our phones is because we are unconsciously scanning for danger, which gives us an innate sense of security. So we're both tribe and night watchman.

The question is, can we do something about our popcorn brain? Yes. But the answer is not what you think: abstinence doesn't help, simply because we can't sustain it in our modern lives. Almost everyone needs their phone again sooner or later. What does have an impact is reducing your dependence on your phone. This means setting digital boundaries. For example, leave your phone outside the bedroom. This will reduce your stress levels. Not convinced? 62% of people check their phone within 15 minutes of waking up, and around 50% check it in the middle of the night. How healthy is that, do you think?

What else can you do? Take two to four (phone-free!) ten-minute breaks a day, as short breaks have a cumulative impact on your stress levels. Breaks boost productivity, mood and energy levels. One last tip: be aware of it every time you reach for your phone. A good exercise is to note down each time why you're looking at your phone. You'll soon become more aware of your actions and might even stop picking up your phone for no reason, creating healthier boundaries in your relationship with technology.

Busting the myth

That age-old cliché that women are good at multitasking – I'd like to consign it to the realm of myth once and for all. It's true that many women do have a lot of balls to juggle, especially if they have children. From jotting down a shopping list during a meeting to planning a birthday party while getting school bags ready for the next day, they seem to combine different tasks almost effortlessly. It only looks that way. The science is clear: no one is actually good at multitasking, and that includes women. For example, a German study published in PLOS ONE shows that women's brains don't work any more efficiently than men's when they have to divide their attention between different tasks.

What about the younger generation? When I look at (and listen to) the young people around me, they are convinced they can handle six to seven different forms of media at once. Bingeing a TV series while simultaneously TikTokking and Snapchatting... It's easy, isn't it? American psychologist Larry Rosen studied the dynamics of the modern brain, focusing on how young people interact with media and technology. In his research he observed teenagers who, while studying, were also checking their phones, listening to music, replying to messages from friends and scrolling through their social media. All of them believed they could perform these various tasks successfully without their studies suffering. But of course Rosen's research told a different story. EEGs and behavioural observations clearly showed that even the younger generation's brains were not designed to process so many information streams at once. They too pay a high switch cost, which can lead to reduced concentration, slower reaction times and lower productivity.

ATTENTION RESIDUE

One reason we feel so *incredibly* exhausted after a busy day of switchtasking comes down to what we psychologists call attention residue. To illustrate this, let's go back for a moment to Gloria Mark's mental whiteboard. Every time you switch to a new task, you erase the previous one and write new text for the new task on your mental whiteboard. But even after erasing, some faint traces of that first text still remain.

So even though you're working on a new task, your brain still holds a residue of the previous 'text'. This attention residue is not a bad thing per se: it helps you remember things and resume tasks easily later on. If you're in the middle of writing a report and the fire alarm goes off, it's handy that your brain remembers what you were working on once you're back at your desk. The problem is that we use this mechanism all day long. Or rather, we misuse it.

When I was a student, I often didn't know the answer to an exam question right away. So I'd skip it and move on to the next. Countless times, the answer to a question would spontaneously present itself a little later, without me actively looking for it. Why is that? My brain just kept working in the background – like an app on your smartphone. All very nice of course, but by the end of an exam I was often mentally drained.

Of course, it's no bad thing to challenge your brain once in a while, say during an exam. But what if we're doing that all day long? What if we're constantly having to deal with the attention residue left over from the previous task? We lose some of our mental strength with each task. Our problem-solving ability and creative thinking are noticeably impaired, as is our memory. We're so busy switching tasks that our brain has no energy left for creating a memory trail. This has inevitable consequences: people who switchtask are estimated to be up to 40% less productive than those who focus on one task at a time. So it's high time we stopped dividing our attention and instead focused it consciously on one task at a time.

Four energy leaks

Dutch psychologist Mark Tigchelaar links switchtasking to four energy leaks:

1 **Energy loss.** Switchtasking demands a lot of mental energy to constantly switch from one task to another, so it depletes our overall energy levels.
2 **Time loss.** Switching between tasks takes time, which makes us less effective at completing individual tasks and lowers our overall productivity.
3 **Quality loss.** When we're switchtasking, we run a higher risk of errors and poorer quality in our work because we can't devote full attention to each task.
4 **Memory loss.** If we are constantly switching between tasks, we are less likely to process and retain information properly, which can impair our memory and learning performance.

YOUR BRAIN, BEAVERING
AWAY BEHIND THE SCENES

An experiment

Challenge yourself to focus for an hour on one specific thing. Eliminate all potential distractions: block off an hour in your diary, hole up in a quiet room in the office, turn off your email notifications and your smartphone. Really try to get completely into the flow, without constantly worrying about what else is on your plate. It may feel uncomfortable at first, but after a while you'll notice what a sense of calm it brings you. Indeed, you'll not only feel more energetic after an hour, you'll probably also have derived more satisfaction from your work. Then try dividing your whole day into blocks. For example, work on that report for an hour, answer emails for half an hour and then sit in a meeting for an hour without looking at your phone. And don't forget to focus on actually taking a break during your breaks! I guarantee that by the end of the day, you'll feel much fresher than usual. You've discovered a new superpower: single-tasking.

Want to do more single-tasking? If so, it's important to think about why you switch tasks so often now. Why are you distracted so often and so easily? The answer to that question is different for everyone, but we can identify two main types of distraction: external and internal.

External causes of distraction are usually relatively easy to address because they are tangible. Email notifications can be turned off, as can your smartphone. I'll admit it's not easy to eliminate distractions in an open-plan office, but there are options here too. More about this in Chapter 5.

Internal causes of distraction are more likely to go unnoticed and so pose more of a risk to our focus. Our brain likes to be busy and seeks ways to fill a gap. Be honest: if I ask what you've read in the last ten minutes, can you give a detailed answer? I hope so, of course, but chances are that some of it didn't stick. Maybe you were disturbed by an external factor, but it's also quite possible that your own mind was to blame. This is because you can think faster than you can read. Reading speed is around 200 to 250 words per minute, while thinking speed is in the region of 1,400 words. The same goes for speaking: our brain makes connections much faster than we can express them. Luckily, there are tricks to fill the gap productively.

Read a tiny bit faster

Have you ever caught your thoughts wandering off somewhere after reading only a few sentences? A word triggers a whole stream of thought and, before you realise it, you're booking your car into the garage? Of course, you might just be reading a very dull book, but even then you might want to grasp *some* of the content. It might be an idea to try speed reading. By reading faster – using the right techniques – your brain doesn't get the chance to wander off.

It might seem counter-intuitive at first, but when you read faster, you give your brain a chance to focus better. The reason is simple. Reading more words per minute demands more attention from your brain. And paying more attention to reading reduces the influence of other thoughts and processes. That sharpened focus will help you get a better grasp on what you're reading. If you do try speed reading, however, it's important to pause after each page and think about what exactly you've just read. Otherwise you risk the content slipping away again.

Use music to soothe your mind

Another trick to sharpen your concentration is to listen to soothing music, ideally something instrumental. Lyrics can activate the language part of your brain so may be more distracting. And it's best to choose familiar tunes: new melodies trigger your curious brain and are more likely to distract you. The frequency of the music matters too: your brain focuses best at 40Hz. Want some help with your playlist? The Endel app creates personalised soundscapes to suit your current activity: it has soundscapes to enhance your focus, but also playlists that can help with unfocusing.

Get moving

Do you find it hard to concentrate on auditory information? When listening to a podcast or a recording of a meeting, try combining it with a walk or some light exercise such as jogging. But make sure you stick to a familiar route and don't try to set any new PBs. Exercise helps you fill the gap and keep your attention on the task at hand. You'll notice soon enough if you're trying to combine too much. Ever become so absorbed in a podcast while driving that you accidentally take a wrong turn? Or vice versa: ever ended up in heavy traffic and then found you've completely lost the thread of your audiobook because you had to focus fully on the road for a few minutes?

~ 5 MINUTES LATER ~

Doodling does it

Another useful method to help you absorb information is doodling. Maybe you were scolded at school for scribbling aimlessly or drawing in your notebook during class. That teacher had the wrong end of the stick: doodling narrows the gap between thinking speed and reading speed, keeping you more engaged in the lesson. If I see my students doodling, I know they're trying to fill the gap and fix their attention. So we *can* do two things at once? Yes, as long as the two tasks don't interfere with each other. Doodling while listening to a lecture or talking on the phone is not multitasking (because there's no such thing), or switchtasking either. So what *is* going on?

Research among young adults has shown that doodling has a positive effect on listening comprehension. Doodling also turns out to help with information retention: students who doodle remember the main subject matter and relevant details better than students who simply listen. Doodlers also appear to be better at monitoring and processing information.

A plausible explanation for the positive effects of doodling is that it prevents daydreaming and keeps students alert. In listening comprehension, working memory plays a crucial role in converting sounds into words and phrases, and in assigning meaning to those words and phrases. Drawing inferences (using knowledge from long-term memory), monitoring information and understanding content also take place in the working memory. During daydreaming, the student uses the limited capacity of working memory for their own thoughts rather than for processing the spoken text. If doodling can prevent daydreaming, this improves listening comprehension.

Sweep your mind

Another handy tip is a mindsweep. Often when you're focusing you suddenly get an idea. Like a light bulb coming on in your head: "Don't forget to stop by the shop later and buy firelighters." To prevent this idea from popping up repeatedly (and distracting you each time), it's better to write it down. By writing something down, you give your brain a chance to let go of it. There's a good reason why waiting staff write their orders down.

Boxing clever

Timeboxing is a time management technique where you assign specific time blocks to certain tasks or activities. In essence, timeboxing involves planning your day and dividing it into defined periods, setting aside each block of time for a specific task or activity. These can range from work-related tasks to personal activities such as sport or relaxation. Timeboxing can be applied to different aspects of life, including work, studies, household chores, hobbies and personal development. It is a flexible technique that can be adapted to individual needs and preferences.

Single-tasking rather than switchtasking can make a world of difference to our productivity and well-being. If you want to start a task with full concentration, it's important to get into the right flow. Once you've got that flow, it becomes easier to focus on one task at a time. The key question, of course, is how do you get into a flow?

THE ATTENTION RITUAL

Rafael Nadal never just walks onto the court. During each break he sets his water bottles down in front of him in the exact same position, with the labels facing the side he will play on. When it's time to go back on court, he spreads his towel over two advertising boards. Then he gently tugs on the corners to make sure the towel is taut. Next he looks at it again, tugs a bit on the right-hand corner and gives the towel a pat. Then he positions himself at the baseline, ready to receive his opponent's serve.

Top tennis players like Nadal can't afford to spend 15 minutes warming their brains up before they're in the zone. From the moment they arrive on the baseline, they need to be fully focused, ready to send their opponent scurrying to all four corners of the court with a few well-directed strokes. This is why they – and many other elite athletes – use a shortcut called an attention ritual to tell their brains it's time to be 100% focused. When Nadal pats his towel, his brain knows it's serious. "I wish I didn't have them," says Nadal, "but tennis is such a mentally aggressive sport that I do everything I can to eliminate factors that might distract me. My rituals help me to focus during a match."

If you look closely, there's a little of Nadal in each of us. For instance, I have friends who always run a comb through their hair before going into a meeting. Another friend keeps a box of shoe polish in his car, so he can give his shoes a last-minute touch-up before an event. On the one hand these rituals are motivated by social norms, perhaps because we want to make a good impression on colleagues or customers. But they are also crucial in order to trigger a mental click and step into your professional role.

The idea behind an attention ritual is simple: when you want to switch from one task to another, your mind needs to calm down first so it can then refocus fully. Like allowing a bow to relax before preparing for the next shot. In other words, rituals act like a reset button for your brain. They help you clear the noise and renew your mental energy. What exactly you do doesn't matter, as long as you consciously make time for these moments of rest. For example, something I do consistently when giving a lecture is park my car a short distance from my destination. For me, a ten-minute walk is the ideal way to get into the flow right away. When I want to focus on a task at my desk, I turn to Leonard Cohen, whose music always helps me to regain focus. When I listen to his song *Take This Waltz*, the first few notes signal to my brain: watch out, here comes a task that demands your full focus.

By the way, did you know that such rituals are often even more prominent among people who work from home? Many people still believe that homeworkers sit around in their pyjamas all day. But nothing could be further from the truth: full-time homeworkers often take a very organised approach to their working day. They get up at a set time, eat a proper breakfast and dress as if for a day at the office. Even if they see no one else all day, a professional outfit puts them in the right frame of mind to get down to work.

It might sound simple, but a small attention ritual like this really can make a world of difference. As you're combing your hair, polishing your shoes or listening to your favourite focus song, you switch off all the surrounding noise for a moment. So ask yourself if you already have some attention rituals like these and, most importantly, if you can consciously make even more space for them in your life. It's a shame that many people perform their daily rituals without really thinking about them, because that way they lose some of their power. If you perform an attention ritual very deliberately, it will guide your impulses even more effectively towards focus and clarity.

An attention ritual needn't be a big or complicated affair. The crucial thing is that the ritual should mentally prepare you for the task at hand. Even a few minutes can be enough to clear the mental clutter. A ritual is like taking time to focus your camera before pressing the shutter. Be creative and find a ritual that suits you: a short meditation, playing your favourite song or simply letting your thoughts flow for five minutes. There is only one rule: choose something that is unique. If you only ever drink coffee before starting an important task, that could make an excellent attention ritual. But if you guzzle endless cups throughout the day and usually round off a nice meal with an espresso, drinking coffee is not unique enough to get you into the flow.

Go with the flow

I talked about flow in Chapter 2, but I want to mention it again here because flow is directly related to switchtasking: it's important to learn to recognise when you are in a flow and when your focus starts to wane. It could be signs personal to you, such as realising that your mind is beginning to wander from what you're reading, or external stimuli. The key thing here is not to set unrealistic expectations for yourself: even a well-trained brain can only stay in the flow for 90 minutes and maintain full focus for up to 4 hours a day. So it's not at all unusual for your flow moments to be short at the outset. The good news, though, is that you can improve them with exercises. Luckily, focus is not a static concept.

CHAPTER 5

ENTER OPEN-PLAN OFFICE, EXIT FOCUS?

It's a scene familiar to us from films of the 1990s: row upon row of office workers sitting at computer screens in their tiny cubicles. Our initial response is to ask how can you ground yourself there, in such a cramped space with barely any room to move? And what about social contact? In the intervening decades we've seen a complete turnaround: gone are the cramped cubicles, to be replaced by open-plan offices and flex spaces.

An open-plan, flexible office space seems fun and dynamic at first sight, but in practice the fun is soon over. Working in an open-plan office is a concentration killer. People soon became nostalgic for their tiny enclosed cubicles. Okay, it was a lot less sociable, but at least you got your work done and didn't go home with a pounding headache.

Scientific studies have shown that employees working in large open-plan offices with lots of other people are generally less satisfied with their work environment. They experience too much distraction and stress. Lack of concentration is the main problem. This is underlined by a recent survey of over a thousand Belgian office workers conducted by Antwerp Management School. Only 56% of respondents said they were able to concentrate well enough.

Maybe you too sometimes sit at a flex desk in the middle of a noisy office where even noise-cancelling headphones are no help. So should we do away with open-plan offices?

OPEN-PLAN OR UNPLANNED?

I often spar with Jo Peters, the man behind design consultancies Deusjevoo and UPspace, about whether and how open-plan offices can work to our advantage. Because there's no avoiding the open-plan office nowadays. For the time being it doesn't look as if companies will be building new offices on a large scale, so we'll still have to find a way to reconcile these open-plan offices with our focus.

Open-plan offices were a perfect fit with the 'new work' concept and 'activity-based working'. The idea was that working together in one big office would increase engagement, promote communication and make it easier to keep everyone in the loop. Unfortunately, no-one considered the needs of the individual employee when designing these spaces. This had serious consequences: there is a growing body of hard evidence to show that working in an open-plan office is actually harmful. So is there nothing positive about an open-plan office? Yes, there is. It's the most cost-efficient way to accommodate people, but that's about the only benefit.

Putting a towel down

So an open-plan office doesn't encourage us to work flexibly? The answer is simple: no. Flex-working usually only creates more stress. Humans are creatures of habit. It all sounds great in theory: everyone gets to choose a place to work every morning. But what happens in reality? People like to sit in the same place every day. And what do you get then? A situation like the old chestnut of holidaymakers getting up with the lark to bag a sunlounger by the pool. People arrive at work earlier to reserve the day's spot in advance – beside their favourite colleague, near the coffee machine, by the window – and claim their working territory. It won't surprise you to learn that this behaviour causes stress levels to peak first thing in the morning. And team spirit to plummet.

SO WE WANT STAFF TO BE ABLE TO CONCENTRATE AS FULLY AS POSSIBLE. WHAT ARE YOUR IDEAS?
WE PUT EVERYONE TOGETHER IN ONE BIG ROOM!!!!!!!

"HAVE YOU GOT A MINUTE?"

"Busy, busy, busy." It seems like the mantra of the 21st century. Ask a business leader how their work is going and nine times out of ten you'll get the busy-busy-busy answer. But if you follow up by asking what exactly they did that day or who they spoke to, chances are they won't be able to come up with an answer. An exaggeration? This is precisely the story Jo Peters told me when he realised, ten years after founding Deusjevoo, that the company's growth had stalled. He was working flat-out, wasn't he? Yes he was, but he suddenly realised he'd been running to and fro for days, multitasking as he went. For example, if he was called to reception he'd be accosted every few steps on his way there – through the open-plan office – by people asking if he could "spare them five minutes". Time and time again. He couldn't get any work done, as he was being repeatedly taken out of focus. The question was, what could he do about it?

At first, he started working harder. He took work home with him, worked late into the evening and went to bed still high on adrenaline. Soon he fell into a vicious cycle, like a whirlpool dragging him towards an inevitable burnout. But luckily he managed to turn the tide.

Jo's story is sadly no exception. Many other business leaders and employees are constantly taken out of focus throughout the day. Unsurprisingly, working like this is not only counterproductive but also bad for our physical and mental well-being.

One of the related and seemingly positive side effects of dashing around constantly putting out fires is that we get rewarded for it with a shot of dopamine. So we're all too happy to be distracted by those easy-to-catch rabbits, such as 'five minutes to answer an email', checking the interaction on a social media post or supplying the right answer to a colleague's 'highly pertinent' question. An open-plan office piles on countless sources of distraction. According to Jo, we are taken out of concentration every two minutes on average.

A colleague walking past, another on the phone, the photocopier buzzing... There are stimuli everywhere. This is actually a form of multitasking too, as your senses are constantly receiving something new to process. A noise. A smell. Someone passing by. In other words, our senses receive constant input and our brain becomes overloaded.

SET BOUNDARIES

To stop sounds or noise destroying your concentration, you can of course work in a quiet room (if there *is* one in the office) or invest in noise-cancelling headphones. These help you shut out distracting noises and focus better on your work.

But headphones don't solve everything. Humans are social creatures and in an open-plan office you're also likely to be distracted by a colleague popping across with a non-urgent question or for a friendly chat. Before you know it, ten minutes have passed and you've forgotten what you were doing. Setting boundaries helps, both social and project-related. Ask your colleague to give you half an hour to finish an assignment. Tell people you prefer to receive non-urgent questions by email so you can answer them in non-focus time. And if colleagues are holding a team meeting at their desks, be bold and suggest they might use a meeting room.

It's true this might feel a bit uncomfortable at first, but keep in mind that your colleagues may also be looking for ways to maintain their focus. If you state your boundaries in a firm but friendly way, they are sure to understand. And who knows, you might inspire them in turn to act a little more boldly when their own focus is disrupted.

Make elephant time and brain parties a fixture in your organisation

Much better than declaring your need for focus time on an ad hoc basis is to carve out a place for elephant time in your team or organisation. We urgently need to remould our offices into brain-friendly workplaces. Peace and quiet is an absolute minimum requirement. The workplace should go back to resembling a library: a quiet space with every opportunity for focus. Interaction with colleagues remains important, of course, but ideally that interaction doesn't happen in the same space.

A brain-friendly space brings immediate benefits. According to neuropsychiatrist Theo Compernolle and his book *Brain Chains* it improves productivity by 30–40%, reduces error rates by around 50% and cuts stress levels by half. These are not made-up numbers but figures based on scientific research.

To achieve a truly brain-friendly workplace, we need to make collective agreements. You can start small, for example by agreeing on specific signals indicating that you don't want to be disturbed right now. For example, you could agree that wearing your headphones means that questions can wait. Some companies have taken up my elephant metaphor in a very visual way. Staff literally put a little elephant on their desk if they don't want to be disturbed.

Set a good example and respect your colleagues' quiet time. If possible, make collective agreements: if the whole team works on their elephant in the morning from 9 to 11, chances are that everyone will be able to do so undisturbed. But keep an eye out: if you see someone approaching a colleague who is deeply absorbed in work, you could head them off and kindly ask them to come back later.

Still finding it hard to organise collective elephant time? Try holding brain parties at regular intervals. Three times a day, lamps are switched on in the office, and that means silence. Give it a try: there may be some initial resistance, but after a few months you'll notice that it's become a habit and the place will naturally fall silent.

DIFFERENT TASKS CALL
FOR DIFFERENT SPACES

So does that mean it has to be all-change all the time? No. Some teams work together almost constantly, for example in communications, sales, logistics planning or a newsroom. Here precisely the opposite is needed: the workplace is *the* place for interaction, so you need to provide spaces that encourage it. In such situations, though, it *will* be important to create focus spaces nearby.

There is no one-size-fits-all solution. The physical layout of your offices will always have to be customised to some extent. Every company is different. And even within a company, there can be huge differences between departments. Copy-pasting the layout for several floors on top of each other isn't a good idea in any case. You need more diversity in your workplace than you might think at first glance.

Don't decide overnight: ask plenty of questions and be prepared to make adjustments if necessary. Only then will you create a human-based workplace that truly places the employee at the centre. For each space, look at the mindset needed to achieve the desired results. Then you can make targeted choices giving employees every opportunity to align their behaviour with that mindset. Is the mindset focus? Great, then the key is to minimise distractions. Is it co-creation? Then you'll need a completely different working environment.

Jo Peters distinguishes four different types of spaces (associated with four core tasks) that are needed in almost every company:

- *Focus space.* Employees need constant access to a physical space where they can work with 100% focus. If you're a brain worker, this quiet space should be your basic workstation. That doesn't mean having to sit on your own in a room where you could hear a pin drop. It's okay for a phone to ring or a coffee cup to tip over, but there are limits. According to Jo Peters, ideally you should have only six to eight people in a space.
- *Break space.* A bowstring can't stay taut all the time. To focus well, it's at least as important to unfocus. So you also need proper break spaces, such as a cosy coffee corner and a nice lunch room. The coffee corner is perfect for informal discussions, while the lunch room can serve as a relaxed place to chat. You can even turn the lunch room into an informal meeting place, reducing the need for formal meeting rooms. And why not have a grand café: a place with a laid-back atmosphere where multiple conversations can go on at once?
- *Communication space.* Create communication spaces where you can hold a proper discussion. Whether it's a team talk, a one-to-one meeting or a consultation with HR. It's vital to have somewhere suitable for an in-depth tête-à-tête. Holding team calls can be great for communication, but it does require a different office layout. Especially in an open-plan office, people often hate team calls because they can be so disruptive. Even if you wear headphones, everyone can still hear what you say. If three people are on a call at the same time, it drives their colleagues crazy. Companies do usually have a few larger meeting rooms, but they quickly get booked up. It's better to aim for more smaller spaces with good conditions for video calls. This includes flattering lighting and a stand to put your laptop on so the other person doesn't have to look straight up your nostrils.

And of course let's not forget a stable network and a functioning microphone and speaker.

- *Co-working space.* Finally, you also need spaces where you can work together and co-create. Think of brainstorming sessions, group meetings, training courses, you name it. Ideally, opt for flexible furniture that can be moved or switched out depending on the activity. Other essentials are a whiteboard, touchscreen, smartboard or post-it wall. Agree to tidy up as much as possible after a meeting so the next group can start with a clean slate. A good tip is to invest in curtains. These are ideal for acoustics and you can quickly hide all sorts of things behind them so you don't get distracted during a meeting by random stuff that's of no use to you at the time.

The cathedral effect

The cathedral effect is a concept that suggests that the height of the ceiling influences our thought processes. Spaces with higher ceilings, such as cathedrals, are associated with more abstract and creative thinking, while spaces with lower ceilings promote more detailed, more analytical thinking. This observation has its origins in evolutionary neurobiology – the study of the nervous system and how it has adapted over time to various environmental factors.

Scientific studies such as those by Joan Meyers-Levy and Juliet Zhu have shown that even small differences in ceiling height can contribute significantly to different cognitive processing styles. Higher ceilings activate abstract thinking, while lower ceilings encourage detailed and focused thinking.

This finding suggests that people can strategically choose their working environment based on the type of cognitive task they want to excel at. In practical terms, for example, you could reserve rooms with higher ceilings for creative work at certain times of day. Analytical work may be better suited to lower-ceilinged environments.

You can also apply the cathedral effect by controlling the height of your visual world, for example by wearing a hoodie or hat that limits your field of vision, effectively creating the effect of a lower ceiling.

"Staff are perfectly capable of booking a meeting room if they want to work in peace for a while, aren't they?" This is a comment I often hear when giving training courses. Especially for smaller companies, it's not always easy to provide different spaces for different tasks, but with a little creativity it needn't be too expensive. Companies are free to set their own emphases, of course: for example, some companies need more focus space than others. But if you really want to get the best out of your staff, it pays to invest in a good mix of these four types of spaces. Be sure to take the individual needs of your employees into account. The following anecdote from Jo Peters sums it up well for me: "We have two staff members who both get easily overstimulated, each with a different job content. One is an accountant, the other does mostly creative work. At one point they asked if they could sit together in a small room because it was quieter there and they could concentrate better. We saw to that right away, of course. This is precisely what we should be aiming for: we need to look at what each individual needs in order to do their job to the best of their ability. We need to stop classifying people according to their range of duties."

A good mix of the four types of spaces, geared as closely as possible to the needs of each individual – that's what we should be aiming for. Jo Peters is doing pioneering work here. Still too few managers are willing to ask their staff what kind of space they need. Yet it's the only way to create offices that are friendly to our brain. As this is a book about focus, the rest of this chapter looks mainly at how we can make space again – both literally and figuratively – for deep work.

WITH YOUR BACK AGAINST THE WALL

You'll have noticed yourself that one workplace is not like another. Sometimes you sit down somewhere and instantly feel: no, I can't concentrate here. Whereas a bustling coffee shop feels like somewhere you can get straight down to work. I'm afraid I can't give you a checklist for the perfect focus spot, but there are a few basic conditions. A vital one is that you need to feel safe.

Remember the sympathetic nervous system from Chapter 3? Constantly scanning your surroundings for danger? An easy way to soothe it a little is to sit with your back against the wall. This gives you a good overview of your surroundings and no one can sneak up on you from behind. Not that our workplace is full of dangers, but our primal brain thinks it is, as Lily Bernheimer points out in her fascinating book *The Shaping of Us*. Lily Bernheimer is the founder of Space Works Consulting and works closely with architects, designers and businesses to create working environments based on our psychological needs. She says we can concentrate better and consequently perform better if we are in a place where there's no risk of a sudden ninja attack. And let's not forget that people need privacy, so they don't like someone peering over their shoulder at their screen.

A room with a view is also a plus: people with a nice view are said to be 6 to 12% more productive than those without.

I've already mentioned that I'm not a big fan of hot-desking, where no one has a fixed workspace and you have to find or even fight for a seat every day. I do understand why companies go for it, because the freedom of choice encourages a degree of autonomy. But people are creatures of habit and tend to feel safer if they have a permanent place to sit. Flexiplace working or hot-desking works for only 5% of employees. For everyone else, it's a – to quote Jo Peters – hellhole, so really not recommended. Surveys conducted by UPspace around hot-desking show that barely 3% of employees would choose it if specifically asked where they want to work.

By the way, it's a good idea to give employees as much say as possible about where they want to work, precisely because a productive workplace is highly person-centred. What one person perceives as safe, another may find boring and uninspiring. We all have the same brain (except we don't), remember?

The open-plan office as a place for focus

Can you focus properly at your desk? Or do you seek out a quiet place for that? If so, you're not alone: most companies are committed to having quiet spaces within the open-plan office, whereas they should actually be doing the opposite. Your basic office space should be quiet so you can do focused work there. Then you need additional break-out rooms where you can confer, relax, celebrate the signing of a crucial deal, and so on.

FOCUS IN A SPACE WITHOUT WALLS?
YES, YOU CAN!

FOCUS BOOST 1   *Eliminate your personal disruptors*

The first question to ask yourself is whether the space you are in is the direct cause of your lack of focus or whether there's something else going on. Be honest: are you bothered by external disruptors or are you mostly distracted by emails and personal messages? The solution is just as simple: turn off all notifications, log out of all unnecessary apps and browsers, clear your desktop and only have one task or project open at a time. And most importantly, put your phone away.

"Yes, but what if someone has an urgent question? I'll need to answer them!" Make clear agreements with colleagues: if there is a fire, they can call you. If an answer can wait a while, an email or a message in the team chat will suffice. Then you can answer emails in bulk after your focus time. Be equally strict when it comes to your partner and children: specify when you're available and at what times of day you're not to be disturbed. Sending that shopping list to your partner can probably wait until your lunch break.

And what about music? Music is a very personal thing. Some people can work with loud music blasting out from the speakers, whereas for others a door opening and closing is enough to break their focus.

The open-plan office: a place to connect

Let's not forget that an open-plan office environment also has its advantages. Working in the same space as others can provide much-needed social control and motivate you to stay focused. Even more importantly, people value connection and collaboration in the workplace. An open-plan office facilitates this connection, precisely because people can find each other easily. This contributes to a positive, feel-good working atmosphere. It also explains the growing popularity of co-working spaces and coffee shops that attract remote workers and freelancers seeking to counter the isolation of working from home.

FOCUS BOOST 2 *Tame your mailbox*

"You have 42 unread emails." If you check your mailbox again half an hour later, it's gone up to 65. How do you get through your work if you're constantly distracted by an annoying 'ping' or receive a text notification of an email with 'urgent' in the subject line? Back when email really was a novelty, we couldn't get enough of it. That's nice, someone getting in touch! Now we regard our mailbox – much like meetings – as a necessary evil, but one that constantly takes us out of focus.

First of all, are these emails all really so urgent? No. If something is truly urgent, people will come to you or call you. If the office is on fire, you don't send an email, do you? Jo Peters told me that some time ago, as an experiment, he set up the following automatic response: "Thanks for your message. It may take 24 hours for me to respond. If it's really urgent, ring me on my mobile number." You've guessed it: he didn't get a single call.

Some email hygiene tips

The first rule of email is that it is NOT for urgent communication. In addition:
- Ban CCs and BCCs. CC is just a way to lend an email more weight vis à vis the outside world. CC only if that person really needs to be kept informed.
- Don't attach files of 16 or more pages to your email with the accompanying message: "For info." No one wants to or has time to read all that. Just say what you expect from your staff: "In paragraph 3, I want a yes or no answer to the customer's query."
- Can you resolve it yourself? Do that first.

FOCUS BOOST 3 *Hold smart meetings*

Meetings are a thorn in the side of almost everyone at work. Hardly anyone enjoys them, just ask around. The following tips are nothing new but apparently they still bear repeating. So here we go:

Gauge the length of a meeting accurately. If you need 15 minutes, only book 15 minutes and don't let Outlook tempt you into blocking a full hour. Finished early? Then close the meeting.

Prepare for meetings. Ideally, a meeting should have a clear agenda so that other attendees can also make the necessary preparations.

Arrive on time. Nothing is more annoying than a colleague who rushes in ten minutes late, expecting his team members to give him a summary. Your time is precious, but so is that of your colleagues.

FOCUS BOOST 4 *Tidy up*

Chaos on your desk? One person likes to play desktop archaeologist and happily embarks on a quest to unearth that document they need. Another swears by a pristine desk with everything in its place. Pen here, coffee mug there, computer screen tilted at precisely 20°.

Chaotic types are only too keen to quote Albert Einstein to defend their messy desks. Einstein is said to have wondered: "If a cluttered desk is a sign of a cluttered mind, of what, then, is an empty desk a sign?" Unfortunately, science says otherwise. Want to be more productive and creative? Then tidying and organising your workspace really is the first step. A cluttered, disorganised workplace can be distracting, which leads to stress and a lack of focus.

Start right now by removing all items that don't belong on your desk or in your workspace and putting them somewhere else. Get some digital rest too: tidy your files and put them in folders so you can find them again quickly.

FOCUS BOOST 5 *Human-centric lighting*

Working by the glow of a single light bulb or getting a splitting headache from harsh artificial lighting? I don't need to tell you that poor lighting can be a focus killer. But did you know you can also use lighting in a very targeted way to boost your focus? Light has a big impact on our waking and sleeping states. More and more offices are taking advantage of this, adopting a principle called human-centric lighting. The lighting in the office should follow the rhythm of the day.

In the morning, pluck the light from the sky

First and most importantly, natural light is always best. If possible, position your desk near a window. Natural light not only boosts your mood but also reduces eye strain and headaches. The best option is exposure to natural sunlight (ideally between 30 and 60 minutes after waking). Nothing can match the natural energy boost provided by sunlight, with its broad spectrum of light waves that directly influence your biological clock and energy levels. The more sunlight you get, the higher your performance.

Bear in mind too that sunlight through a window is 50 times less effective than direct sunlight, so make sure you go outside regularly to recharge.

If direct sunlight is not an option in your office, it is best to go for warm or cool artificial lighting that mimics natural light. Avoid bright fluorescent lighting, as it can cause fatigue and headaches. Take it as read that light is essential though, because it stimulates the melanopsin ganglion cells in the lower half of your retina. It is these cells that boost your alertness and improve your cognitive performance. Especially in the dark winter months, light is a lifeline. It not only encourages much-needed focus but also stimulates the release of neurotransmitters such as dopamine and noradrenaline, while regulating your cortisol level, which is essential for a healthy stress response.

If you can, mix and match different light sources such as desk lamps and overhead lights. Add a ring light or a bright LED lamp for an optimal lighting environment. And consider using blue light. This stimulates the activity of the melanopsin ganglion cells, resulting in increased alertness and cognitive performance.

After midday, dim the light

A bowstring can't stay taut all the time. As mentioned earlier, unfocusing is at least as important as focusing. Natural light (or artificial lighting approximating to natural light) can boost your cognitive performance, but it's just as important to let your brain unwind afterwards.

After an intense focus peak, it may be a good idea to dim the ambient light for a while. Don't go and sit in total darkness, as you may end up in a dip you might struggle to get out of. Dim the overhead lights and opt for warmer lighting closer to hand. This time of day sets the tone for creative and abstract thinking, opening your mind to new possibilities and innovations.

So different types of activity call for different lighting. A tip from Deusjevoo/UPspace is to have break-out rooms with lighting in different colour temperatures. In any case, it makes for a refreshing change. They even have an area where you can choose cool (focus!) or warm (creativity!) lighting or a combination of the two.

Around 4 to 5pm is the time to reduce exposure to light – especially high-energy blue light. This is because blue light keeps you awake. Switch to light sources with a softer, warmer glow that prepare you for a restful evening. Also dim the screens of your devices to reduce the impact of blue light or, better yet, set your smartphone aside as much as possible.

You'll notice that these adjustments not only make a big difference to your creative thinking and productivity throughout the day, but also dramatically improve your sleep.

What about evening and night work?

People who work in shifts need to stay alert in the evenings and at night. So they need light, but ideally you should avoid excessively bright light during night work. Too much bright light can significantly lower melatonin levels and disrupt your circadian clock. The effect could be likened to jetlag. And depending on how long it goes on for, that can affect sleep, metabolism and overall well-being. It's true of course that bright light during night work can help you to stay alert. So it's a matter of striking the right balance.

Occasional night owls – such as students pulling an all-nighter – may well benefit from a night of bright light. Although I'd quickly add that studying through the night doesn't yield better results in most cases, quite the contrary. Your brain needs processing time and starting an exam well-rested holds out better chances of success.

FOCUS BOOST 6   *Add a splash of green*

Various studies have shown that plants can reduce stress, improve concentration and promote overall well-being. They also improve the air quality and moisture balance in a room. Succulents, spider plants and monsteras make good choices as they are low-maintenance and thrive under artificial light.

If living plants are not your thing, you can also opt for artificial ones. Even fake plants can have a positive effect on your stress levels and so boost your concentration. Just make sure they are good quality and look realistic, as cheap plastic specimens can have precisely the opposite effect. And yes, even a print or picture with a plant design has been found to have a positive influence on stress levels.

FOCUS BOOST 7   *It's all about ergonomy, stupid*

There's nothing more annoying than a chair that doesn't feel right or leaves you bent and broken after a day's work. Sitting at a desk all day puts a lot of strain on your body and an uncomfortable position can lead to physical strain and reduced productivity. And constantly wobbling to and fro because you can't find the right sitting position is not only bad for your focus, it's also distracting for your colleagues. So it's essential to design a workstation that is both comfortable and ergonomic.

The basics for a comfortable workstation? A sturdy chair that can be ergonomically adjusted to your needs, with good lumbar support, adjustable height and armrests. This keeps you sitting comfortably and maintaining good posture throughout the day.

The height of your desk is important too. Ideally, your desk should be at a height that allows you to work comfortably without bending forward or putting strain on your arms. If your desk is too low, consider using a footrest to raise your feet and keep your knees at an angle greater than 90°.

Apart from desk height, another crucial factor is the distance between keyboard and monitor. Your monitor should be at a comfortable viewing distance, with the top of the screen at eye level or slightly below. Your keyboard and mouse should be at a height that allows your elbows to rest comfortably by your sides.

Finally, take a critical look at the overall configuration of your workstation. Constantly turning your neck to look at your screen? Consider using a monitor arm that allows you to adjust the height and angle of your screen.

By taking time to design a comfortable and ergonomic workstation, you not only reduce the risk of physical strain and discomfort but also heighten your productivity, precisely by working in a space that supports your body and mind.

FOCUS BOOST 8 *Stand up!*

Do you know the expression 'sitting is the new smoking'? It stems from the observation that most of us have ended up in sedentary jobs over recent decades. The rise in computer work came at the expense of manual labour or jobs that required us to move around much more. Computers and robots are taking over. And where robots twist and turn with elegant precision, we sit. Gaze at the screen, slumped in a chair. This is not good for our health, let alone our focus.

In his book *Breath: The New Science of a Lost Art*, science journalist James Nestor talks about how damaging all this computer work is for our health. It can lead to screen apnoea, a term coined by former Microsoft vice president Linda Stone. Stone noticed that, as she sat at her laptop opening emails, her breathing became shallower, sometimes to the point of holding her breath. It's a situation you might recognise: you have multiple tabs open, text messages pinging, an urgent email demanding attention... We are assaulted by constant stimuli and our brain is not designed to handle them.

According to Nestor, scientists and doctors believe that screen apnoea is a manifestation of our body's stress response. Our nervous system constantly scans incoming stimuli and decides which of them we should regard as threatening, and the mental effort required triggers a whole range of physiological processes. Our breathing and heart rate slow down, allowing our body to concentrate and devise a plan of action. A bit like a scaled-down version of the fight-or-flight response. Imagine a predator stalking its prey: just before it pounces, it stands stock still and breathes more shallowly. The same thing happens when you get a message.

You might be wondering what the link is to loss of focus or attention? To answer that, I'll return briefly to Chapter 3. There I explained how your brain goes into survival mode at the first sign of danger, taking your neocortex out of action. But you need that very neocortex in order to do focused thinking. Moreover, if your nervous system is on constant alert for a whole working day, you'll be exhausted by the end of it, even if it doesn't feel like you've had a stressful day.

Research shows that people who alternate between sitting and standing during the day generally perform better and are healthier than those who sit for extended periods of time. Hurray for sit-stand desks then, though unfortunately they are still in the minority in the workplace. Strikingly, even in workplaces that do have sit-stand desks, they are not always used. Much of this has to do with the wrong choice of seat. So adjust your desk to the right height for standing work and choose a desk stool with foot ring rather than a classic office chair. If your desk is properly adjusted, your eye level remains the same whether you're standing or sitting, making it easier to alternate between the two.

If a sit-stand desk is not an option, it's important to stand up frequently. Making phone calls, for example, can be done standing or walking. Why not walk-and-talk with a client for an informal discussion? And as unfriendly as it sounds, it's better for your colleague if you leave his forgotten copies at the copier. You're doing him a favour: research suggests that even a modest reduction in daily sitting time has significant benefits. Less sitting leads to less neck and shoulder pain, better health, more vitality and better cognitive performance.

As in so many things, balance is key: people who have to stand all day will testify that this isn't great either. The ideal situation is to spend around half of your working time sitting and the other half standing.

Want to take things a step further? You might consider an active workstation with a treadmill or cycling desk, although obviously this isn't feasible for everyone. Movement while working can improve your attention and cognitive control. But note that for tasks that require sharp verbal memory, sitting or standing is better than moving. So if you're consulting with colleagues as to how to tackle a complex project, it's best to do it sitting down. Brainstorming, on the other hand, can be done while standing, though of course you mustn't forget to write down all those brilliant ideas.

Embodied cognition

Our brain isn't separate from our body. We really shouldn't underestimate the effect of movement on our thinking. A key term here is embodied cognition. What do we mean by that? It refers to the fact that our brain not only works on its own but is also heavily influenced by our body and the world around us. For example, if you're holding a cup of hot coffee in your hands, the heat and weight of the cup will influence not only your hands, but also your thoughts and feelings.

Embodied cognition emphasises this interaction between body and mind. By the way, this interaction is driven not only by direct physical sensation. If you think of the concepts 'high' and 'low', for example, you'll unconsciously stretch your neck when thinking of something tall, like a skyscraper. This physical aspect is linked to your mental representation of height. In addition, we often use physical metaphors, such as a 'warm person' or a 'cold look', that show how our physical experiences influence our social interactions.

FOCUS BOOST 9   *Adjust your screen to the right height*

Did you know that the positioning of screens (phones, tablets, computer screens, etc.) is not only important for good ergonomic posture but also plays a crucial role in how alert you are? The human visual system is pretty complex. Our eyes are connected to our brain through a network of neurons. Part of this network is specifically focused on directing our eye movements. Some neuron clusters are responsible for 'looking down', while others are concerned with 'looking up'. Interestingly, these movements have an effect on our alertness. When we look down, our brain seems to get a kind of signal to relax. It's as if it's saying: "Okay, now it's time to chill for a while." When we look up, this activates a different part of our brain that is more concerned with alertness and focus.

In simple terms: looking up = being alert; looking down = being relaxed. So a quick win is to position your screen at eye level or even slightly higher. Your neck and shoulders will thank you too!

Apps can help too

If you still struggle to stay focused despite all these tips, there are plenty of apps that can help to eliminate distractions. So you don't suddenly end up with 20 productivity apps on your phone, I'll start you off with two recommendations. Focus@Will offers music that helps you to focus, while the Forest app gamifies productivity by encouraging you to stay focused for a certain period of time.

FOCUS BOOST 10   *Change your environment*

An effective way to boost your focus is to change your working environment regularly. After two to three hours of working in an open-plan office, for example, you could relocate to a meeting room. By doing this you create a fresh environment that can trick your brain into feeling as if you haven't been working for very long. Something else that has a positive impact is changing your sitting posture. By adjusting your position and changing your surroundings, you shift stress to different parts of your body and reduce physical effort. This can help to reduce fatigue or restore concentration after a period of intense work activity.

You can adopt a similar approach at home: after a few hours' working at your desk, go into the living room and continue there. This change of surroundings gives your brain a fresh stimulus that can help reduce fatigue and prolong your concentration.

The idea behind this strategy is that, by changing your working environment, you can alter your perception of time and encourage your brain to focus again. It's a practical way to heighten productivity and combat the lapse in concentration that often occurs after working for a long time on the same task or in the same environment.

CHAPTER 6

WE NEED TO MEET AGAIN

In many respects, we've never had it better than we do today. In his book *Ten Reasons to Look Forward to the Future,* Swedish journalist Johan Norberg points out that, in terms of health, wealth, freedom, security, nutrition and education, we are living in the best era of human history. I agree with him on that. Despite the major global challenges on our plate, if we compare our modern lives with those of our great-grandparents it's clear that the world itself and humanity have advanced in leaps and bounds.

Especially in the last few decades, the world has seen dramatic change. Much of this is due to the rise and revolutionary impact of the World Wide Web. When the internet became commonplace in the early 2000s while I was a psychology student, I was perpetually amazed at how easy it was to locate a scientific paper deep in the digital recesses of a library in France. Before, you'd have had to physically comb the library archives for your material, but now suddenly all it took was a few clicks.

Since then, the pace of digitisation has accelerated rapidly. Thanks to the internet and the thousands of digital applications developed in its wake, we are now connected to everything and everyone all over the world. Our circle of friends fits in our pocket. We swipe to arrange our love lives and make wild online plans that we cancel just as quickly. We are hyper-connected, but we seem much less able to truly connect with each other.

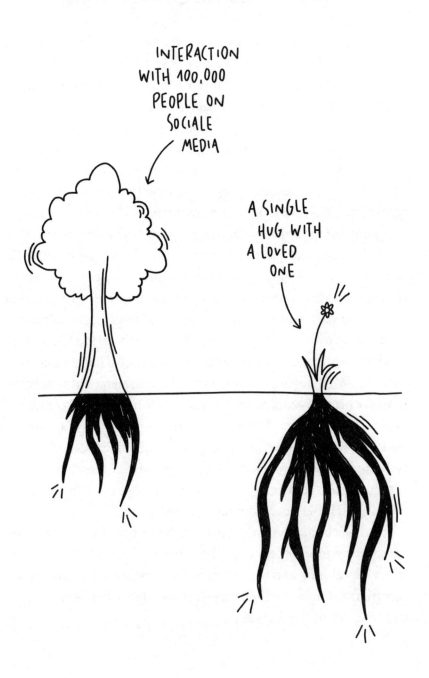

MAKE AUTHENTIC CONNECTIONS

You could have thousands of online friends and followers, collect hundreds of thumbs up with every post, but still feel lonely and alone. Virtual friendships may inject a dose of happiness hormones, but they don't really make you happy.

It will come as a surprise to no one that interacting with countless followers on social media cannot hold a candle to a single intense hug with a loved one. Your follower numbers may be impressive and 'wow' a lot of people, but the genuine wow feeling you experience from a personal relationship is unmatched.

Human beings are actually a highly complex system of countless connections: our cells, body and mind constitute a network that is in constant conversation. It is no exaggeration to say that connection is the backbone of our existence as a human species. The power of connection goes well beyond our inner workings: it extends to our relationship with the world around us and our social life. We nurture close ties with others, with our environment, with nature and even with our own thoughts. And all of that is essential for our well-being.

You've probably experienced it yourself: when you feel connected to others, you flourish. You feel supported, understood and appreciated. And when you feel at one with your surroundings and nature, you experience a deep sense of harmony and fulfilment. Even cultivating a strong connection with our own thoughts and feelings can help us find inner peace and contentment.

For true connection, it's crucial to be in touch with your own purpose and meet others from there. But let's be honest, in a world where algorithms and technologies are constantly angling for our attention, it's sometimes challenging to embrace the here and now and truly connect with others.

Let's not forget that connection is not only a human need but also a vital ingredient for our long-term resilience. When you strengthen your focus, it not only changes your approach to yourself and your tasks, but also has profound effects on your interpersonal relationships.

Connecting with others can significantly enhance your work. Recently, I travelled to Athens for a lecture at an international conference. As my hotel was hard to reach, I opted for a taxi. I was rewarded with a remarkable conversation with the taxi driver. He showed an interest in who I was and what I did, and in return shared his life story with me. He told me he regretted not having a diploma and therefore motivated his daughters to pursue higher education. Despite not having his dream job, he maximised his experience by engaging in meaningful conversations and learning from his customers worldwide. His approach was admirable, centered on building connections. It's a perfect example of how to make the most of each day, no matter your profession.

When you pay genuine attention, or when you elevate your focus, you are better able to be in the here and now, which is essential for building strong relationships. You are more present, more empathetic and better able to understand the needs of others. This leads to deeper, more fulfilling interactions and strengthens the bonds you have with those around you. Improved focus increases your ability to communicate effectively. You are able to get your thoughts and feelings across more clearly, which minimises misunderstandings and promotes harmony in relationships.

THE HAPPINESS HORMONE

When you experience a feeling of connection with another person, something happens in your body: the happiness hormone oxytocin is released, which in turn stimulates the production of serotonin, often called the body's 'feel-good' chemical. Oxytocin and serotonin can reduce stress, anxiety and even the risk of depression. Serotonin is also associated with digestion, appetite, sleep, memory and sexual health.

But to achieve a true connection you need to feel safe and secure. If you feel anxious or afraid, your brain immediately switches to survival mode and the space to make connections disappears. If you feel insecure, for example at a party where you don't know anyone, it is difficult to connect. Conversely, if you feel at ease, conversations come naturally. By gaining more control over your brain's response, you are better able to form meaningful relationships with both yourself and the world around you. Luckily, you can influence this yourself to some extent by activating your prefrontal cortex. This region of the brain regulates emotion, promotes rational thinking and helps you maintain a feeling of calm.

SPOTLIGHT ON FOCUS

All well and good, but why am I writing about connection in this book about focus? There is indeed a link, and it's this: when you feel connected to people, your brain calms down. Your brain's safe mode takes you out of survival mode, towards a feeling of relaxation where it opens up to more experiences and connections. This also improves your ability to concentrate and pay more attention to what is going on around you. It enables you to form meaningful relationships, both with others and with yourself.

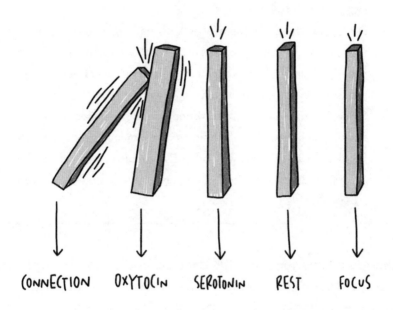

CONNECTION   OXYTOCIN   SEROTONIN   REST   FOCUS

Connect with your focus

Here are some easy tips and exercises you can use to sharpen your focus. The good news is you can start using them today.

- **Gratitude.** If you think intentionally about things, people or experiences you are grateful for, it gives your brain a boost. This not only strengthens your rational thinking skills but also reduces stress and anxiety, leaving you in control and less prone to negative impulses.
- **Deep breathing.** Deliberate deep breathing tells your brain that you are safe, allowing you to live in the here and now. Deep breathing slows down your heart rate and lowers your blood pressure, so you automatically experience a sense of calm.
- **Smile for true connection.** When someone smiles at you, it makes you happy. It's as simple as that. Smiling is a fun and effective way to connect with others. A genuine smile can create a domino effect of positivity and contribute to a feeling of true connection.

"Huh? But didn't you say in the last chapter that working with colleagues in the office is often a real focus killer?" Yes, it is a catch-22 in a sense: it's hard to achieve true focus in the office for many reasons, which is why we'd all prefer to work at home more often. But by doing that we are also missing out on connection, with inevitable consequences. There is a solution: hybrid working can combine the best of both worlds. Provided we do it right, that is. And that's often where the proverbial shoe pinches.

HYBRID WORKING IS HERE TO STAY

It was British statesman Winston Churchill who, in the aftermath of the Second World War, once uttered the famous words: "Never let a good crisis go to waste." His implication was that every crisis gives rise to extraordinary developments. At that time, it was the founding of the United Nations. A few years ago, another worldwide crisis prompted us to scrutinise the way we work. During the COVID pandemic, offices stood empty and most people were forced to work from home. For some that was a curse, for others a blessing. Leaving personal preferences aside, the COVID crisis and the associated working from home have led us to look at work very differently nowadays. First of all, we have found that we don't necessarily have to be in the office in order to work properly. Working from home didn't turn out to be a licence for employees to shirk or cut corners, as many employers had feared. Deadlines were met, the figures stayed healthy and the work got done. With the huge bonus that many employees felt a lot less stressed and were happy to be able to manage their work–life balance more easily to suit themselves.

Even post-pandemic, hybrid working still has many supporters. My own belief is that the future of work will be hybrid, combining the best of both worlds. It's true that some issues did surface during the peak of working from home. For example, we no longer had to factor in travel time and the inevitable traffic jams, so we were able to cram our schedules with back-to-back online meetings. Even now, people who work from home often don't take a break between meetings. We schedule successive video calls while monitoring our emails and company chat. If we can, we put our microphone on mute and listen with half an ear to what our colleagues are saying while also finishing that urgent report. We're sprinting from one mental marathon to another, something a top athlete would never do. On the contrary, after each effort they would take some quiet time to loosen up and relax their muscles for a while. But what do we do? We stretch our mental muscle to the limit, on the basis of willpower and personality.

This way of working is not sustainable. We need to learn how to do hybrid working right. That means finding a good balance between what we do in the office and which tasks we plan to do at home.

WORK DONE AT HOME IS SOMETIMES DONE BETTER

Working from home offers many advantages in terms of both professional and private life, that's an inescapable fact. Many employees say that working from home regularly makes it a lot easier for them to keep all the balls in the air. Less time spent travelling means less of a rush at home in the mornings and evenings, for example. But we also tend to be a lot more productive at home than at work. If you've read the previous chapter on open-plan offices, I probably don't need to explain why. At home, it's much easier to tailor your surroundings to your needs and create the ideal focus zone. Though this doesn't seem to be equally obvious to everyone. Precisely because we're working from home much more often, the boundaries between home and work are becoming increasingly blurred. Flip the laptop open on the coffee table in the evening? Can do. Quick phone call while making a start on dinner? No problem.

This flexibility offers many advantages, but we still need to be careful not to lose focus. In his latest book *Trends in the Transformation Economy*, author Christophe Jauquet says that the number of activities we engage in at home – from working to relaxing, from cooking to exercising – only seems to be increasing. In the midst of

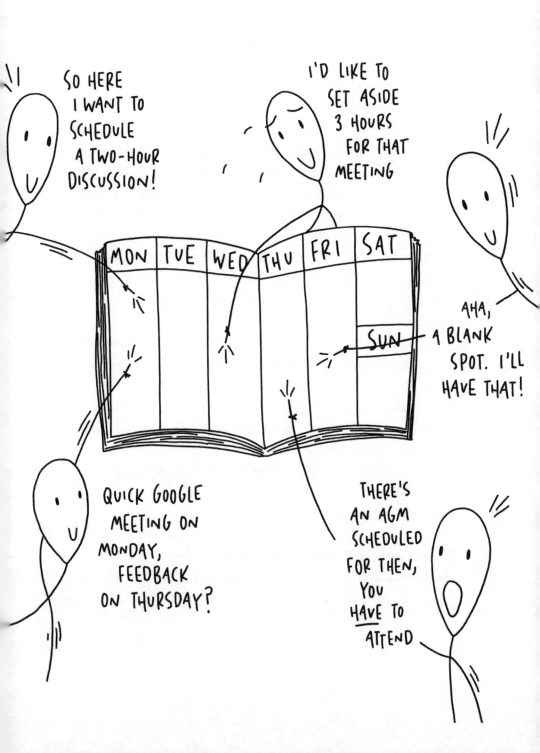

all this activity, it's not always easy to find ways to focus on what we are doing without being constantly distracted. So there's a need for clarity and focus at home too.

Just as we need to think about our office set-up, we also need to think about our workstation at home. Here too, we need to create an environment that supports our focus and clarity. IKEA's *Life at Home Report* stresses this point: people want to have control over their living space so they can focus on what really matters.

Not everyone has the luxury of dedicating a separate room at home to each activity. For most of us, it's a matter of making smart use of the space available. It's no coincidence that furniture giants are focusing increasingly on flexible designs with multiple functions. After a long day's work, you might want to fold up your desk so your work is out of sight. Maybe you'd like to quickly convert your home office into a mini yoga studio so you can relax after work. And so on. It's about our home being a place where we can escape the chaos of the outside world. A place where we can find clarity and focus, but also relax.

Our home is often the ultimate place to unwind, recharge and just be ourselves. Luckily, there are many things you can try at home to increase calm and avoid stress and anxiety. Consider using calming colours that promote a sense of comfort and inner peace, or interior design styles such as Japandi that create a serene and safe environment. I'm also seeing a return of nature into our homes, with a stronger focus on plants and trees, organic materials and fragrances, and large picture windows offering beautiful views of the outdoors.

Even in the midst of all this burgeoning activity, our home remains a haven of relaxation. People are becoming increasingly aware of the importance of a tidy and organised living environment. Indeed, research has shown that a tidy home can reduce feelings of depression, while a cluttered environment can actually exacerbate stress. Isn't that what we're all striving for: a place where we can find clarity and peace?

HOME ALONE

That shiny working-from-home medal – more rest, more focus – also has a reverse side. As much as it may sound like a tempting alternative to the daily commute and the survival of the fittest in a noisy workplace, working from home also has a significant drawback. At home, you're usually on your own.

Working from home is a bit like being a fish on dry land: you keep breathing for a while, but in the long run you dry out. Yes, by working from home you do avoid the traffic jams. Yes, you enjoy the flexibility. But when you work alone, you don't connect with other people. Not with your colleagues, not with your organisation and not with yourself.

In the same way as fish thrive in a nice convivial pond, so we humans thrive in an environment where we feel connected. We recharge while chit-chatting around the coffee machine, brainstorming in the conference room and celebrating shared successes in team meetings. Moments of connection are essential in order to forge strong bonds with your colleagues. No connection, no commitment. Without commitment, you feel less secure. And by now you should know that feeling safe and secure is a key prerequisite for focus.

In my opinion, focus and connection are inextricably linked. They are like a pair of ballroom dancers keeping each other in balance. You need both in order to be productive. You need both in order to feel good.

WORKING IN THE OFFICE

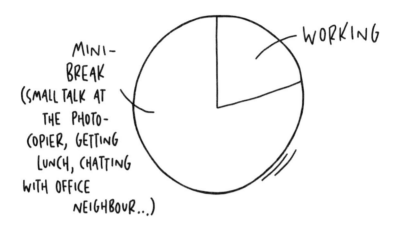

WORKING

MINI-
BREAK
(SMALL TALK AT
THE PHOTO-
COPIER, GETTING
LUNCH, CHATTING
WITH OFFICE
NEIGHBOUR...)

WORKING AT HOME

WORKING.

AAAAH!!

WORK CAN TAKE MANY FORMS: MIX IT UP!

On paper, hybrid working appears to be the solution. You work part-ly at home, partly in the office. This way you have the best of both worlds: you stay connected with your colleagues, but you can also do deep work in the peace and quiet of home. At the office you work on projects in interaction with others, while at home you add the finishing touches solo. Sounds perfect, doesn't it? So why is it that many people sigh when I mention hybrid working?

The main reason is that we can't or won't make clear decisions. We schedule online meetings while working from home and try to get focused work done in the office. So hybrid working tends actual-ly to bring us the worst of both worlds.

The big advantage of hybrid working is that you can plan your own individual schedule. Except we too often forget that such sched-ules don't work if you don't first make very clear agreements with your team. If you've planned a homeworking day full of deep work, phone calls from colleagues will undoubtedly be very distracting. But on the other hand, it's irritating for them if they urgently need info from you in order to finish a report.

Hybrid working as a team is a real challenge, one you will only conquer if you communicate openly and clearly, for example about what you expect from each other and when. It really is worthwhile agreeing as a team on who is available and when, and in what cir-cumstances someone can or can't be disturbed. Sometimes it's in the little things. Think carefully about who you cc in an email, for example. Group non-urgent questions together in an email that you send at the end of the working day, so your colleague doesn't feel compelled to answer each question right away. An invaluable tool here is a team charter, a document that clarifies expectations and lays down clear guidelines for working together. By making these joint agreements, you keep everyone on the same page and support each other in delivering your best work.

Even then, it remains challenging for many people to guard their boundaries. People-pleasers mainly want to make others feel good, and that often comes at the expense of their own time, let alone mental well-being. Fortunately, there are different – and gentle – ways to define your boundaries. For example, by giving subtle hints, blocking time in your schedule or having an open conversation with your team members and stating your preferences clearly. The goal? To create an environment where everyone feels heard and respected.

It can be interesting to get together with the whole team to do an analysis based on what we at Better Minds at Work call synchronous and asynchronous work. Synchronous working means getting team members to work on the same task or project at the same time, regardless of physical location. For example, this could mean being present at the same time during a video meeting, working together on a document in real time, or consulting each other regularly for input or feedback. In asynchronous working, on the other hand, team members don't have to work concurrently on the same task or project. For example, they might work on a project at different times or communicate through written messages that don't require an immediate response.

Once you have a clear understanding of which tasks are synchronous and which are asynchronous, the next step is to agree an effective schedule that works for everyone. For example, we reserve Monday mornings for asynchronous work and block time in the afternoon for synchronous tasks. The ideal is to work synchronously at the office and asynchronously at home, but that's not set in stone. The fact that the whole team can work asynchronously on Monday morning is enough in itself to provide sufficient calm and focus. The same goes for synchronous tasks: of course it's nice to hold real-life team meetings in the office, for example, but the most important thing is to schedule them in synchronous working time. That way, no one has to interrupt their focus time for a meeting.

Is hybrid working right for you?

Maybe you're wondering if hybrid working is right for you? It's worth really taking the time to think about this and not jumping straight in at the deep end. Where do you belong?

Is it at the kitchen table, alone with your laptop, or is it in the bustling energy of the office, surrounded by team mates? It's important to strike a healthy balance between working from home and being in the office. Reserve working-from-home days for tasks that demand focus and concentration, but also plan regular office days to strengthen bonds with your colleagues, collaborate on projects and preserve a sense of connection.

By being intentional about hybrid working and leveraging the benefits of both working from home and working in the office, we can avoid the drawbacks and create a balanced, sustainable way of working that supports both our individual needs and the needs of our organisation. And bear in mind an important piece of wisdom: a virtual meeting is no substitute for true connection.

CHAPTER 7

IT'S NOT JUST COMPANIES THAT NEED A MISSION STATEMENT

Let me begin this chapter by setting you a little assignment: write down how your morning went, from the moment you woke up to the moment you arrived at work and started your day job. How many conscious decisions did you make? Or did you just follow your regular routine?

We are often unaware of it, but we live on autopilot more than we think. Or would like. In the morning, you automatically reach for your phone to scroll through your social media, brush your teeth while your mind is already in the office, and get dressed without noticing what you're actually putting on. Maybe you laid out an outfit the night before, but did you do it mindfully or did you just throw together some things you thought would match?

Your conscious awareness? Maybe you left that out this morning. You probably acted without paying conscious attention to your actions. A bit like driving a car: starting the engine, changing gear, applying the brake... you haven't thought about it in a long time. You've mastered the actions.

Have a think about it: how much attention do you pay to your behaviour? I'm not talking about social situations, but the way you move through your day. How many automatic actions have you mastered in your life so far? Which actions do you still do very consciously? And are you genuinely happy with that? Or do you want to get back in control of your own life?

YES YOU KAHN!

Once I was visiting a company where the copier had been out of action for weeks. People were grumbling about it, waiting for a technician, thinking it wasn't their job to fix it. Within five minutes, I'd pulled out the paper jam and got the thing working again. This may be a simple example, but it was indicative of the prevailing culture in the company: the staff were stuck in a passive role. "Everything was better before. It's not my responsibility. My boss wouldn't like it." Statements I unfortunately hear all too often in the workplace. Many people don't take ownership of their situation. They see themselves as having little autonomy because they're not managers, for example, which locks them into a passive role. Taking responsibility yourself gives you a sense of power.

You *can* transform from a victim of your situation to a hero in control of your own life. A first key step is understanding why you so often fall into automatic actions. Why do you make one decision and not the other? To explain this, I'd like to borrow from the Dual Systems Theory of Nobel laureate Daniel Kahneman and his fellow psychologist Amos Tversky. This theory made a significant contribution to our understanding of human cognition and decision-making.

The Dual Systems Theory states that we have two main ways of thinking and decision-making: a fast system and a slow system.

System 1 could be seen as the brain's autopilot. It is intuitive and works without us consciously having to think about it. Say you need to do a quick sum, such as 2 + 2. Before you even think about it, the answer springs to mind. This kind of quick thinking is useful for everyday tasks such as recognising faces or responding to dangerous situations. So while it's certainly a valuable system, it can also lead to quick, impulsive decisions taken without our full awareness.

System 2 is the opposite. It is slow, deliberate and takes effort. This is the kind of thinking we use for complex tasks that require more attention and concentration, such as solving a complicated problem or making strategic decisions. When we really need to concentrate and think deeply, System 2 comes into play.

It's important to understand the difference between these two systems of thought. People often believe they are making a conscious decision, but they forget that their thinking is largely influenced by System 1. In complex situations, this can lead to mistakes and misconceptions.

Say you need to make an important financial decision. If you act quickly, based on your initial impulsive reaction, you run the risk of making mistakes. If you take the time to think calmly and look at the situation from different angles, you can make better-informed decisions. In other words, if we understand System 1 and System 2, we can better navigate the complexities of life, make better decisions and gain more control over our thinking and actions. This enables us to live more consciously and purposefully, which may ultimately lead to greater success and satisfaction in various aspects of our lives.

A good example that nicely illustrates the battle between Kahneman's two systems of thought is the bat-and-ball puzzle. Let's think it through together. A bat and a ball together cost $1.10. The bat costs $1 more than the ball. So the question is, how much does the ball cost? Quick, intuitive thinking (System 1) leads many people to the obvious answer of 10 cents for the ball. But you've guessed it: that answer is wrong.

The slower, more conscious system of thought (System 2) kicks into action later and reconsiders the initial impulsive decision. Through logical reasoning, you realise that if the ball costs 10 cents, the bat should cost $1.10, giving a total of $1.20, not $1.10. So the right answer is that the ball costs 5 cents.

Kahneman points out that even highly educated people such as Harvard students often give the intuitive, wrong answer, showing that this phenomenon is not associated with lower intelligence. On the contrary, it's very common among people who are highly intelligent. What the puzzle does highlight is the importance of consciously checking our intuition and activating our slower, critical thinking system in order to draw accurate conclusions.

What am I thinking right now?

We spend too much time living on autopilot. That's because we do most of our thinking on autopilot. It's impossible to put an exact figure on it, but let's assume we have between 40,000 and 60,000 thoughts every day. Most of these dissipate quickly or drift by like clouds. But sometimes thoughts linger and drag us with them into a negative narrative. In the car, for example, people are often a much more negative version of themselves than if you just met them on the street. That's because we get bored easily in the car, so our prefrontal cortex is less switched on. Our stress system can take over and negative thoughts are more likely to get the upper hand. The result? Our primal brain makes us swear and gesture at drivers around us.

It often happens to me in the supermarket. I had another incident recently: once again, I'd chosen the wrong queue at the checkout. One negative thought after another invaded my brain. "Typical, why does this always happen to me? Why can't that old man do his shopping some other time? Doesn't he have plenty of time during the day? And that cashier doesn't look very enthusiastic, no wonder the queue isn't moving." I was shocked to have such ungracious thoughts about someone who was just doing their job. I decided to silence my primal brain and triggered myself by saying:

"Now you're going to make that cashier laugh." It took a few jokes, but I left the shop in a very different mood than if I'd given my primal brain free rein, probably resenting the whole place and everyone in it.

You've probably had this experience of being dragged down by a spiral of negative thoughts. Actively ask yourself: what am I thinking about right now? What are the thoughts under the surface that define my behaviour, my beliefs and the way I live my life? This technique is known as WAIT, which stands for What Am I Thinking? When you ask yourself this simple question, something unusual happens in your brain: you shift your attention from System 1 (your autopilot) to System 2 (your prefrontal cortex). The prefrontal cortex offers you a helicopter view and reminds you that whether or not one checkout queue moves faster than another is purely a matter of statistics. Of course you don't always choose the slowest queue. You just don't notice the times you're out within five minutes, because our primal brain is geared to remember mainly the negative things.

Most of the time, our thoughts wander without us even noticing. By actively intervening regularly and asking yourself "What am I thinking right now?", you create a meta-awareness: you identify the streams of thought circling around in your head. In this way you are not a slave to your thoughts, but can consciously choose to adopt a different, more positive mindset.

SHORTCUT TO THE WRONG ANSWER

The bat-and-ball puzzle is a nice illustration of the way that our brain sometimes takes intuitive shortcuts in order to solve problems. People tend to reduce the complexity of the problem by ignoring the more-than formulation and focusing on a simpler version. This makes them think the bat costs $1, rather than $1 more than the ball, which makes the maths a lot simpler. If the bat costs $1 and the total cost of ball and bat together is $1.10, then the ball must cost 10 cents.

Does this mean that intuition is always misleading? Research suggests otherwise. In an interesting experiment, Bastien Trémolière and Wim De Neys studied people's responses to similar problems where intuitive answers conflicted with their existing knowledge. The researchers asked participants to answer two variants of the bat-and-ball puzzle, but this time with expensive cars taking centre stage. In one version, participants were asked the following question: "A Rolls-Royce and a Ferrari together cost $190,000. The Rolls-Royce costs $100,000 more than the Ferrari. How much does the Ferrari cost?" In the other version, the question was: "A Ferrari and a Ford together cost $190,000. The Ferrari costs $100,000 more than the Ford. How much does the Ford cost?"

What was the outcome? In the second version of the problem, where the intuitive answer conflicted with what they already knew about the cost of a Ford, participants were more inclined to think more deliberately and solve the problem correctly. This suggests that people think more carefully when their intuitive answers contradict their existing knowledge.

To sum up: intuition is not always wrong, but it's important to be aware of situations when it can mislead us. By thinking more consciously and checking our intuition, we can improve our ability to solve complex problems and make better decisions.

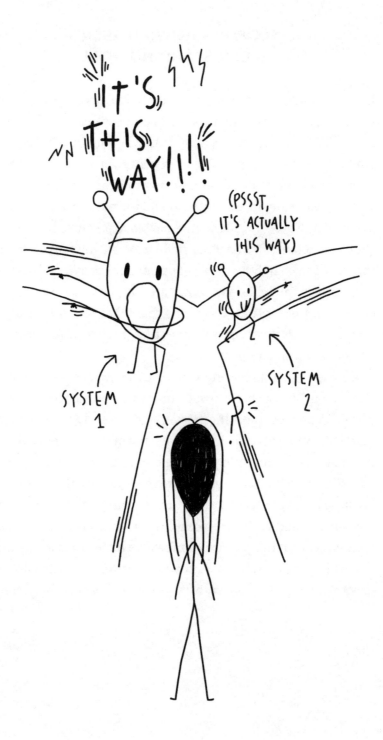

SLOWING DOWN DOESN'T MEAN STANDING STILL

Imagine you're driving your car and need to make a tricky left turn. Most people will stop talking at this point because they need to concentrate fully on the manoeuvre. Or maybe you turn the radio down when looking for a parking spot in a city you don't know? Both of these are examples of our second system in action.

When we really focus on a problem, various processes take place in our body. These include changes in blood pressure, heart rate and skin conductance. It's as if our body is preparing for the challenge that lies ahead. In other words, System 2 takes quite a lot of effort. And unfortunately, human beings are a bit lazy. So we prefer to rely on System 1, our intuitive thinking that takes very little energy. Except this makes it very easy to stay stuck in existing patterns, so you end up living on autopilot.

A golden tip to put System 1 out of action for a while? Consciously slow down. Let's go back to your morning routine we talked about earlier. Tomorrow morning, try very deliberately to break it. Don't reach for your phone as soon as the alarm goes off, but take a few minutes to breathe calmly in and out, and consciously plan your day. While brushing your teeth, take the time to really feel the toothbrush against your teeth. Feel the invigorating jets of the shower and enjoy the moment. Choose clothes from your wardrobe that reflect your mood and that you feel comfortable in. In other words, instead of rushing mindlessly through your morning, consciously choose how to do each task and pay attention to every decision you make.

Kahneman in practice

Kahneman's work is of relevance not only to psychologists, but also to anyone striving for a more fulfilled and conscious life. How to apply it in your everyday life? Here are a few examples:

- It's likely that you always take the same route to work or to visit family. You could almost find your way there with your eyes closed. The surrounding area? You stopped noticing that a long time ago. But what if you decide to try a different route? You'll suddenly see different things, hidden spots will reveal themselves and you'll feel more connected to your surroundings. Breaking a routine can lead to more variety.

- Or what about your social media behaviour? Often we scroll mindlessly through our feeds, without really thinking about the impact of the information we're consuming. But what if we become aware of our online habits and decide to limit our time on social media? You could selectively follow only those accounts that inspire you and bring positivity, making your digital environment a source of joy and motivation rather than stress and negativity.

- Kahneman's findings can also help us to communicate better and connect with others. Instead of giving a knee-jerk response to conflict or tension, we can consciously choose empathy and understanding. By listening to what the other person has to say and seeing things from their perspective, we can reduce conflict and deepen our relationships. It's interesting to step out of our comfort zone and gain new experiences. By consciously choosing challenges and adventures, we can grow as individuals and enrich our lives with valuable memories and opportunities for learning.

ENVIRONMENT DRIVES BEHAVIOUR

Changing your behaviour is a good way to give System 2 more of a look-in, but it's not the easiest way. Daniel Kahneman therefore recommends also taking a close look at your environment. When I was writing this book, for example, I worked on it mainly at home. But since distraction is always lurking there too, I sometimes relocated to a nearby co-working space where I wasn't confronted with an unmown lawn, a full laundry basket or the dishes left from the night before. Working elsewhere provided a different kind of focus, and even though it was sometimes a bit noisy where I was sitting, I still got a reasonable amount of work done.

Changing your environment is a very different approach to the focus issue compared with what you usually hear. Taking a rational perspective, you might choose to make plans, set goals and reward achievements. Kahneman doesn't think much of that whole rational approach. He believes that the secret lies in changing your environment, adapting it in such a way that it becomes very easy to exhibit desired behaviour. The easiest way to change your behaviour is by creating circumstances that make your desired behaviour easier and more natural than it is now. Want to exercise more? Leave your running shoes by your bed and put them on as soon as you get up. Want to become more customer-focused? Reserve a spot in the office for a client meeting every Friday. Want more team work in your company? Change the workstations so that teams sit together more.

FROM KAHNEMAN TO COHEN AND BACK

I enjoy listening to Leonard Cohen. His music – and his voice in particular – promote a sense of calm after a busy day. Cohen combines poetry with beautiful songwriting, and he also has something to say. In the 1960s he wrote an experimental novel called *Beautiful Losers*, in which he asked: "How can I begin anything new with all of yesterday in me?" This was a reference to his love life. Cohen moved fairly easily from one casual relationship to another, often with considerable overlap. But the quote also applies nicely to habits in general. The idea that the past can hinder us from starting something new is something a lot of people can identify with.

If you want to break free of your habits, it can be difficult to change something you have done for a long time. We are often held hostage by our routines, even when we know they don't serve us. The key is not to be too strict: you can't change overnight, and nor do you have to. Just as the loves of Cohen's life overlapped, the same thing can happen with our habits. You can develop new, good habits while old, bad habits lie dormant for a while. And that's okay.

Changing habits is a process of trial and error. It doesn't matter if you fall, what's important is to keep standing up again. Your past doesn't define who you are or what you can achieve. You always have the freedom to choose new paths and form new habits, no matter what happened yesterday. So if you weren't perfect yesterday (and who ever is?), you can start again today. See past mistakes and missteps as learning opportunities to help you move forward with renewed energy and determination.

MICRO-HABITS, MACRO-CHANGE

"You're only one decision away from a completely different life." So many motivation workshops would have us believe. As if you can just 'decide' to change your habits. B.J. Fogg, author of *Tiny Habits*, doesn't believe that. Of course, you do need to take a first step sooner or later. So wanting to change is good, but at some point the enthusiasm you felt on starting a new challenge starts to wane. Somewhere between the pleasure of starting something new and the satisfaction of actually managing to finish a task, we give up. Why? Because we can't keep going forever based solely on willpower. Willpower is like a muscle: sooner or later it gets worked to exhaustion. And when that happens, our good intentions melt away like snow in the sun.

Just as Rome wasn't built in a day, you can't expect to change ingrained habits overnight. It takes time to change a pattern or develop a new habit. One thing that benefits me enormously when I want to acquire a new habit is not setting myself the goal of seeing immediate lasting results. Rather than saying "I'll do this from now until the end of the year", I choose to re-evaluate every three days. In this way, I set shorter, achievable goals and don't get overwhelmed by my own desire to do everything perfectly, right from the start. Lots of little steps often take you further than one big step. Or as James Clear writes in his bestseller *Atomic Habits*: "What you repeatedly do ultimately forms the person you are, the things you believe, and the results you enjoy... Change your habits and you'll change your life."

But how do we do that? The secret lies in building new routines. To do this, says James Clear, we need four ingredients:

1 *Cue.* A starting signal that tells you it's time to take action.
2 *Craving.* The inner motivation that drives you to adopt the new behaviour.
3 *Response.* The actual action you perform that is prompted by the cue.
4 *Reward.* The satisfaction you feel on completing a task that encourages you to do something again.

You can use these four ingredients consciously if you want to develop a new habit. For example, say you'd like to start your day by taking a short walk. Your action plan might look like this:

- *Cue.* You set your alarm for 6.45am. When your alarm goes off, that's the cue to put on your walking shoes.
- *Craving.* If you want to increase the chances of leaping out of bed as soon as the alarm goes off, it's useful to have a clear idea of your goal. What's your motivation? Why do you want to walk in the morning? Try to put it into words. For example: "I long for the energy I get from a morning walk. I literally want to get a fresh start every day."
- *Response.* As soon as your alarm goes off, put on the sportswear and walking shoes you laid beside your bed the night before. Go outside and stroll around the neighbourhood for a quarter of an hour.
- *Reward.* After your walk, you feel refreshed and full of energy. You're happy to have done something healthy and active when the day has only just begun. This positive feeling motivates you to go for another walk tomorrow morning, reinforcing the habit.

Without these four ingredients, new behaviour will never become a habit. What's nice is that once something *has* become a habit, you do it automatically, without conscious effort. That's what makes habits so powerful. They form the basis of who we are and what we achieve in life.

To repeat, keep it small and simple. Aim for small changes. Don't say: I'll eat four pieces of fruit every day. Do say: I'll take at least one bite of an apple every day. Chances are you'll go on to eat the whole apple. But if you do stop at just one bite, you've still fulfilled your initial intention. The result? A successful experience. And success gives a taste for more. The same applies to focused work. Choose a small, achievable goal. If you resolve to focus on a task for three hours, you'll feel as if you've failed if your attention wanders after a few minutes. Maybe you simply won't make a start next time.

This is not a plea to go easy on yourself. Of course you can challenge yourself. Only when you step outside your comfort zone is growth possible. But growing in small bursts will take you further down the road than painful growth spurts. A one percent improvement – repeated every day – leads over time to huge changes in your life. Yes, it may take a while, but the results are worth it and they last. If you adjust your course by only half a degree, you'll be in a very different place after ten years than if you'd just kept going.

Good habits, however small, can make that one percentage point of difference. Instead of focusing on an abstract, intimidating goal, we can routinely carry out small actions or behaviours that consistently improve our productivity and well-being.

Anchor your habits

Micro-habits can lead to meaningful and lasting changes in your life. Whether it's drinking a glass of water before breakfast, taking a minute every now and then to meditate or do some deep breathing, stretching at your desk every hour or writing down three things you are grateful for every night. All of these are small adjustments that boost your well-being in both the short and the long term. But the key question remains: how do you maintain these new habits – however small – in the longer term?

If these new habits always have to be performed consciously – in other words, if you have to keep deciding to do them – you will never persevere with them. They need to become instinctive. So find some anchor points. By this I mean link your new habit to a familiar routine, so an existing routine can trigger the new behaviour. A few examples:

- As soon as you wake up: drink a glass of water or do a brief meditation.
- In the shower: take a moment to express gratitude or repeat a positive affirmation.
- Just after breakfast: do some quick stretches or visualise your goals for the day.
- After a phone call: take a few deep breaths to relax or jot down a task for later.
- After booting up the computer: plan your tasks for the day or make a to-do list.
- On closing the front door: remind yourself of a positive mantra or set an intention for the day.
- Before or after a meal: take a moment for mindfulness. Reflect on what you're thinking about right now, do a short body scan or write in a gratitude journal.

You could also consider reversing the process of building micro-habits by replacing small, non-productive habits you already have with healthier alternatives. For example, instead of checking your phone as soon as you sit down, you could choose to take a few deep breaths first or focus on your posture.

One last tip: think back to the via negativa from Chapter 2. Instead of adding new habits, see if you can cut out any small bad habits. You don't always have to replace them with a new habit.

THERE'S NOISE ON OUR LINES

Imagine you need a new smartphone. You've done your research and know which model you want to buy. On stepping into the shop, you're overwhelmed by the vast selection. Even though you know what you want, a sea of new possibilities suddenly opens up. That smartphone at $450 does look good. And that refurbished handset? Slightly older, but quite a bit cheaper than the one you had in mind. Your brain gets confused, you start having doubts and you just can't decide. In the end, you go home without a new phone.

Maybe you too sometimes find it hard to make decisions – ones that appear easy at first glance? You're not alone. Daniel Kahneman has a name for it: it's 'noise' that makes you doubt yourself and stops you being decisive. By becoming aware of this 'noise' and taking specific steps to reduce it, we can make better decisions. How do you do that?

"Bringing discipline to judgement." According to Kahneman, it all comes down to disciplining yourself and taking the time to make a good decision. One approach is to draw up a proper checklist. For example, what criteria in terms of feasibility, cost and impact should the new strategy meet? After drawing up a checklist, you can seek input from specialists and professionals. Their differing perspectives will enable you to identify possible blind spots and make a better-informed decision. Then take the time to analyse and evaluate every aspect of the situation. Weigh up the pros and cons and make a preliminary decision based on the available information. But that's not the end of it. Before finally taking the plunge, take some time to test out your preliminary decision. Look again at all the information you've gathered and ask if there are any factors you have missed. You might even decide to have a trial run to see how the new strategy works in practice before implementing it fully.

This is a process of disciplined judgement that demands focus and dedication but can lead to consistent and effective decision-making. By taking the time to analyse thoroughly, gather input and test your decisions, you can reduce 'noise' and ultimately make informed decisions that increase your chances of success.

DRAFT A PERSONAL MISSION STATEMENT

Every manager or CEO understands the importance of a mission statement. It contains the essence of what the company stands for and what it does. Its aim is to promote company cohesion and coherence. Anyone reading it will know what the company stands for. If you're faced with a decision within the company, you can test out the right option on the basis of the mission statement.

Wouldn't it be nice to have a mission statement in your personal life as well? What matters to you? What do you want to stand for? What are your goals and values? If you want to be in control of your own life, you need to know which direction you want to go in. A personal mission statement can be the vital compass that keeps you on the right course even in choppy waters. Sometimes it means you'll be swimming against the current. But in the words of my colleague Erik Franck: "If you don't change anything, nothing changes." Standing still is not an option if you are striving for growth and change.

Your personal mission statement

Maybe you've already thought about what your values and goals are, but you've never actually done anything with them. So I'd like to invite you to put your personal mission statement down on paper. A suggestion to get you started:

I, [first name] [last name], see my personal mission statement as a concise summary of who I am. It encompasses my core values and aspirations, independent of factors such as where I live, my work or my partner.

My mission statement is an active statement, free of any vague terms such as 'try' or 'maybe'. It clearly reflects my passions and where I get my energy from.

It may feel a bit strange, but believe me: until you put your personal mission statement down on paper, it will remain empty words. It's only when you write it down that it becomes real. So ask yourself what your personal mission is. In which direction does your compass steer you and how does it help you decide if you're still on the right course?

HOW FOCUS MAKES FOR SUCCESS

In 2013, American psychologist, writer and science journalist Daniel Goleman published a fascinating article about focus and intelligence and the extent to which they can influence leadership and affect your personal development. He writes that leaders – though this actually applies to everyone – need to have a great deal of self-awareness, because this is the basis of emotional intelligence.

More specifically, you need to be able to understand and correctly assess your own emotions, strengths and weaknesses, goals and values. Without a healthy dose of self-awareness, it is hard to gauge how you come across to others and how your own emotions influence your decision-making. It's also important to listen to your inner voice, or to internal psychological signals, and then act accordingly.

A good case study is a survey of 118 professional traders and 10 senior managers at 4 investment banks in London. The most successful traders (with an average annual income of £500,000) were not those who relied solely on analysis, nor were they the ones who simply went with their gut. They were those who focused on a whole range of emotions and then used them to assess the value of their intuition. When facing losses, they acknowledged their fears and became more cautious. The least successful traders (with an average income of £100,000) ignored their fears and just carried on, with inevitable consequences. And precisely because they ignored a wider range of internal signals, they ended up being misled. In other words, people who focus on internal psychological processes make better decisions.

But that's not all: in addition to self-awareness, self-control is an essential condition for effective leadership. Self-control, or cognitive control, refers to the ability to keep your attention focused and resist distractions. It's that very focus that forms a crucial part of the brain's executive function and is often mentioned in the same breath as willpower. Cognitive control is important, especially for leaders, because it enables them to pursue goals despite distractions and setbacks. People with well-developed cognitive control can be recognised by their ability to remain calm in a crisis, control their own inner turmoil, and recover quickly after a setback or defeat.

A fascinating New Zealand study nicely demonstrates the importance of cognitive control or willpower. In this study, 1,037 children born in the city of Dunedin in the 1970s were tested for willpower at several points in their childhood. The tests included the famous marshmallow test devised by psychologist Walter Mischel, in which children had to choose between eating one marshmallow now or waiting fifteen minutes and then getting two. Around a third of them ate the marshmallow right away, another third were able to wait for a short while, and the last third held out for the full fifteen minutes.

Years later, when the researchers revisited the study participants, now in their thirties, those who had waited longer for the marshmallow turned out to be significantly healthier, more financially successful and to hold more positions of authority than those who had been unable to wait. In fact, statistical analyses showed that degree of self-control in childhood was a more powerful predictor of financial success than IQ, social class or family circumstances. Walter Mischel later stressed that the way we direct our attention is essential for exercising willpower.

A second key point that Goleman mentions is your ability to focus on others. In other words, what is your capacity for empathy? Goleman refers here to the 'empathy triad':

- *Cognitive empathy* or the ability to understand another person's emotional state and perspectives. If you have cognitive empathy, you are able to see the world through the eyes of others and understand their thoughts, views and feelings. Cognitive empathy requires a degree of self-awareness and analytical skills in order to interpret accurately what other people are experiencing.
- *Emotional empathy* or the ability to sense emotionally what someone else is feeling. You experience the same emotions as the other person, or similar ones, in response to their emotional state. Emotional empathy allows you to feel deeply connected to others and to show empathetic responses that resonate with their emotional needs.

- *Empathic concern* or the action-focused component of empathy. Not only do you show compassion, you also take specific steps to help or support others in difficult situations. Empathic concern means you are able to provide effective support, lend comfort and find solutions to other people's problems.

The empathy triad emphasises the importance of a holistic approach to empathy, involving not only understanding and feelings, but also active engagement and support. For leaders, applying the empathy triad is crucial in order to build effective relationships, improve team dynamics and create a positive, supportive working environment. By using cognitive empathy to understand others better, emotional empathy to connect with their feelings, and empathetic concern to provide practical help, leaders can strengthen their emotional intelligence and improve their effectiveness at leading teams.

Goleman is not alone in this. Many other scientists share his vision and stress the importance of self-awareness in order to understand the emotions of others. See, for example, this quote from Tania Singer, former director of the Social Neuroscience Lab at the Max Planck Society in Berlin: "You have to understand your own feelings in order to understand the feelings of others."

Singer believes that in order to develop emotional empathy you need two types of attention: a targeted focus on the emotions of others (which involves becoming aware of how *you* would feel in that person's situation) and an open awareness of external cues (e.g. facial expression, voice intonation and other outward signs of emotion). If you can integrate these two types of attention, you can show deeper understanding and empathy for the emotional experiences of others.

The higher the status, the lower the attention

Lead by example. A nice summary of what leadership is all about: you set a good example and hope that your leadership style can inspire others and motivate and encourage your staff. Self-awareness, empathy, an open mind – these are the core qualities of successful business leaders. However, research suggests that people's ability to perceive and maintain personal connections exhibits a kind of psychological decay as they move up the ranks and gain power. Dacher Keltner, professor of psychology at the University of California, Berkeley, found for example that higher-ranking people consistently turn their gaze less towards lower-ranking people and are more likely to interrupt or monopolise the conversation. In other words, they pay less attention to the other person, creating a position of power. In a similar vein, you can see how the balance of power works in a company from the way that person A responds to an email or message from person B: the longer it takes for A to respond to B, the more relative power A has. Map response times across a whole organisation and it will give a remarkably accurate picture of social status. Top executives leave emails unanswered for hours, while those at lower levels in the organisation respond within minutes. The point of this box is that where we see ourselves on the social ladder determines the standard amount of attention we pay to others. And that's important, because top managers need to be aware that excellent ideas can also be found in the lower levels of the organisation, not just in the higher echelons.

A third point that Goleman highlights is focus on the wider world. Leaders shouldn't focus solely on day-to-day operations; they also need a broader understanding of the organisation's strategic goals and direction. A sound strategic focus enables leaders to set long-term goals and develop effective plans in order to achieve them. And here too, creativity and innovation are core concepts. Leaders must be open to new ideas, able to challenge existing processes and devise new solutions to problems. Innovative leaders foster a culture of creativity and experimentation within their teams, which can lead to breakthroughs and improvements in the organisation.

Does all of this sound entirely logical to you? It would seem to be a matter of common sense but even now, more than a decade since Goleman published his article, the link between attention and sound leadership is still not fully appreciated. Attention is the basis of key leadership skills such as emotional intelligence, organisational intelligence and strategic intelligence. And it's this very attention that is nowadays under severe pressure. Wherever we are on the corporate ladder, all of us are constantly bombarded with information, leading to sloppiness, good ideas going unnoticed or key information being overlooked. We scan our emails by subject line only, skip voicemails and skim-read memos and reports.

Leaders who take note of these three focus areas and develop them not only start to work more efficiently, but also have a positive impact on their teams and organisations. Self-awareness and self-control lead to better decisions and mastery of emotions. Showing empathy and developing strong relationships leads to a supportive and collaborative environment. And through strategic focus and innovation, these leaders help their organisations adapt to changing circumstances and address future challenges.

PERSONAL LEADERSHIP

Once you know your personal mission, it becomes easier to take ownership of not only your career but also your own life. That ownership extends far beyond simply taking responsibility for your actions. Executive coach Carolien Van Den Bosch taught me the essential skills needed for (personal) leadership. In essence, it's about becoming aware of your choices, identifying your goals and values, and actively steering your life in the direction you envisage. This might include making decisions that are in line with your dreams and aspirations, even if that means stepping outside your comfort zone.

Here too, I'd like to revisit Kahneman's 'slow' system of thought for a minute. If you're living on autopilot, you're steering blindly based on System 1. You're living by intuition. That might sound appealing, but there's a strong chance that at some point you'll become stranded somewhere you really don't want to be.

Personal leadership is only possible if you deliberately engage your System 2 thinking. So, like Kahneman, I advocate consciously choosing our slow thinking system when appropriate. Once again, you can start small. Remember my checkout story from the previous chapter? A simple "what am I thinking right now?" can take you off autopilot and bring you back to the here and now. By creating more meta-awareness – that is, being more aware of your thoughts and internal mental processes – you can regain control of your thoughts and the actions that follow. You'll be able to filter out the noise from your thinking more easily and make more conscious, informed decisions that align with your personal values and goals.

The Great Glass Elevator

Sometimes it's good to gain a little distance. In *Charlie and the Great Glass Elevator* by Roald Dahl, Charlie and his family find themselves in a large glass elevator with the eccentric chocolate factory director, Willy Wonka. Panic ensues, causing Wonka to be unable to press the right button to direct the elevator to the famous chocolate factory. As a result, the elevator propels the entire group into space.

How often do *you* step into a proverbial glass elevator? We're so busy with the rat race of everyday life that we don't usually take time to look at our lives and work from a distance. But we need to do that in order to see the bigger picture. It can be incredibly enlightening to leave the issues of the day behind and step into the proverbial glass elevator.

The further you are away from something, the more you'll be able to see the surrounding bigger picture. That ability makes us unique as humans. This sort of abstract thinking will only become more important in the future. Not only because it differentiates us from robots and computers, but also because it gives us control over them.

The metaphor of the great glass elevator helps you get a clearer picture of various questions that at first glance appear abstract. Want to get a better perspective on your dreams and ultimate goals? Then why not zoom all the way to the top floor? What does the view look like? How do you feel when you're on top of the world? And what do you think of your life when you see it from a distance? If you feel like you're getting bogged down in trivial details, the top floor may give you a better overview of what's important and what's not. But it can also be useful to go down a few floors, for example in order to make some concrete decisions and actually roll up your sleeves.

Stepping into the great glass elevator once in a while helps you become aware of what's going on in your life and what you'd like to change. You can keep your eye on your goals and dreams and track down your 'why'.

Why do you do what you do? It was Simon Sinek who pointed out that we are too often preoccupied with what we need to do and how we're going to do it, but rarely ask ourselves why. In the great glass elevator, you can identify your why. It's a powerful reminder to stay focused on what really matters for your personal growth and fulfilment.

THREE QUESTIONS TO FIND HAPPINESS

Maybe the great glass elevator metaphor still feels a bit too abstract to you? If so, I'd like to give you another tool that I myself use on a daily basis. Every evening, I reflect on the day that has passed by asking myself three questions devised by Dr Luc Isebaer, a respected world authority on solution-focused therapy. His three questions have changed many people's lives for the better, including mine.

The first question is: "What did I do today that made me feel happy or grateful?" This question invites you to reflect on what makes your life meaningful and what brings you satisfaction. This can include relationships, personal achievements, helping others and personal growth.

The second question is: "What did someone else do today that made me feel grateful?" In other words, who added positive energy to my day, how and why?

The third question is: "What did I hear, see, feel, smell or taste today that made me feel happy or grateful?" In other words, go back to the basics, the five senses, and ask how can I consciously perceive these sensations more often in my day in future?

When I started doing this exercise at the end of each day, I noticed that the common thread in my answers often had nothing to do with standing on a stage here or giving a lecture there. It was often the moments with my daughters that lingered: how I took them to school and we told each other jokes along the way or the cosy chat we had just before they went to sleep. I realised that if I wanted to get a better sense of my purpose, I needed to spend more time with them and limit my speaking engagements abroad. Which I did.

These three questions still serve as my compass. They help me to consciously choose a happy life every time and to keep my focus on my goals and values, no matter what's going on in the world around me. Every evening I get the chance to take my life to the next level and to consciously anchor happiness in my life and maintain focus on it.

From victim to hero

You probably know the feeling of being stuck in a spiral of negative thinking. You're convinced that everything you set out to do is doomed to failure and your focus is no longer on your talents but on your limitations.

If you step into the great glass elevator and look at your situation with a slightly broader gaze, you'll probably notice that you're not so much 'limited in your abilities' as stuck in a particular pattern. As soon as you become aware of that pattern and the triggers that send you into that negative spiral, you'll be able to recognise the negative bias promptly in future and respond appropriately. When your colleague asks you for an outside-the-box solution in a meeting, maybe the first thing you think is: "But I'm not creative".

WHAT DID I
DO TODAY THAT
MADE ME
FEEL
HAPPY?

WHAT DID
SOMEONE
ELSE DO THAT
I THOUGHT
WAS NICE?

WHAT DID I
HEAR/SEE/FEEL/SMELL
OR TASTE
THAT I
ENJOYED?

By jumping straight to that thought, you paralyse your brain and prevent yourself from coming up with a brilliant idea.

Here too, it helps to actively trigger your meta-consciousness. If you're constantly thinking: "I can't do this!" or "I'll never be good at this", the simple fact of observing those negative thoughts can call them into question ("Is that really the case?"). Then ask yourself where those thoughts are coming from. Maybe you'll discover that they stem from fear, insecurity or self-doubt.

Once you're able to identify the negative thoughts, you can work actively on reversing these patterns. For example, by replacing them with positive affirmations or by consciously focusing on successes and achievements. Identifying and reversing negative thought patterns is a crucial first step towards personal growth and empowerment. It enables you to define your own mission or goals clearly and to strive actively for positive change in your life. Instead of getting stuck in a helpless victim mindset, you can transform to a hero mentality, where you identify your own power and use it to achieve your goals.

Epilogue

While I was writing the last few passages for this book, Belgium was having – to put it mildly – a wet spring. The pouring rain lent a natural background of white noise that helped me to keep happily working away. Until I started on this epilogue. Suddenly my focus had gone.

"Sum up concisely why you wrote this book", my publisher had told me. But the more I delve into the topic of focus, the more I am convinced that focus is *the* key to a whole range of different challenges we face today. How do you sum up something like that without it sounding like an empty slogan?

I decided to ponder the issue over a cup of coffee. Switching on the radio, I heard a short news item about a company called AFAS Software. Suddenly the jigsaw pieces for this epilogue fell into place. The company management had announced plans to introduce a four-day working week from 2025, with staff retaining full pay. They will get every Friday off and won't have to make it up by working extra hours in the rest of the week. My thoughts flew to Johann Hari, whose book *Stolen Focus: Why You Can't Pay Attention* mentions a New Zealand company that gave its staff more paid free time. The results were promising: teams worked more efficiently and were less likely to get distracted. Their social media use fell by 35%. This drop in screen time resulted in 30% more teamwork and much higher engagement. Employees reported having a chance to decompress, a crucial process that boosts cognitive functions such as decision-making, emotion regulation and planning.

MORE TIME MEANS LESS WORK

Have you heard of Parkinson's law? It's the principle that work expands to fill the time available. In other words, if you set aside two hours for a task that you could actually finish in an hour, it will often take you two hours. The law was originally coined by British naval historian Cyril Northcote Parkinson. And he hit the nail on the head. For example, in a humorous essay for *The Economist* in 1955, Northcote Parkinson wrote about a woman whose only task of the day was to send a postcard. How long does that take? Five to ten minutes. If you're busy, you can fit it in between your other activities. If you have all day, you'll unconsciously spend much longer on the task. You'll spend an hour picking out the perfect card, another half hour finding your glasses or the right ballpoint pen, then 90 minutes writing the card, and maybe even 20 minutes deciding if you need to take an umbrella on your short walk to the post box.

It sounds pretty far-fetched, but this example is closer to reality than you might suspect. The same thing often happens in big companies. For example, Apple delayed the launch of their HomePod as they needed "a little more time" to refine it. Windows kept holding back an expected feature for Windows 10 only to scrap it altogether. The construction of the Sydney Opera House was only supposed to take four years. In the end, it took fourteen. Why? All of it down to Parkinson's Law.

Set a generous time limit for a task and, before you know it, your project will grow arms and legs. Imagine you're a company IT department investigating a pesky bug. In no time at all, you're working on not only the bug, but also a few related problems you encounter along the way. And then you want to get to the bottom of those, which takes you down another side track. This could be helpful in the end, because you might discover something useful you wouldn't have noticed otherwise. But still: the distractions don't really bring you any closer to fixing the original bug, which was the whole point. What should have been a simple undertaking expands to take two weeks.

And that happens in every company, every day. If you've set aside two hours for a meeting and everything has been discussed in an hour and a half, it's a rare person who ventures to close the meeting earlier. On the contrary, various items and topics will come up that may have nothing to do with the meeting, but everything to do with the idea that "we have to fill these two hours, otherwise it's time wasted".

Parkinson's law says that if you are given five days to achieve certain goals, you will use all of that time. By shortening the working week, you challenge employees to complete their tasks within a shorter time frame. The outcome? More focus, more creativity and more productivity.

FOCUS IS THE NEW IQ

The Ancient Greeks had a phrase for it: *panta rhei*. Everything flows, and especially nowadays. We live in what anthropologist and futurist Jamais Cascio aptly describes as a BANI world: brittle, anxious, non-linear and, for many, incomprehensible. In such turbulent times, it is only human to fall back on what feels familiar. Except that's not what we need. The clock stands at five to midnight: to take back control of our brains we need to act now, before we have to set up mass detox clinics to help people regain full focus.

For far too long we've relied on easy solutions to help us keep pace with our increasingly complex world. We've tried to give our over-tired brains a rest by outsourcing various tasks. Tasks we used to

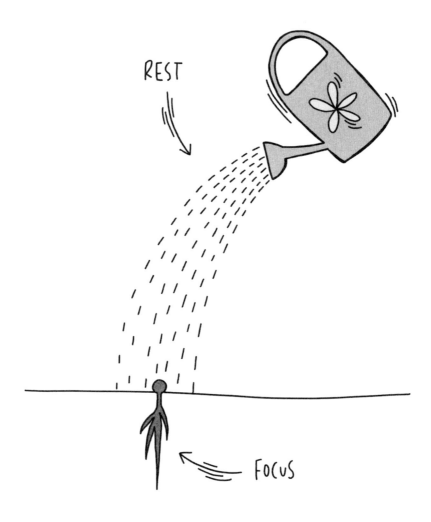

carry out purely on brain power we now outsource to computers, smartphones and AI. Unfortunately, this keeps us spinning in a vicious circle: to give our brains a rest, we create all sorts of new tools, but these in turn create additional stimuli.

The time for quick fixes is over. We need to muster the courage to completely reshape the way we live and work if we are to keep our feet in these turbulent times. That means putting our brain at the centre of everything we do. In my first book *Better Minds*, I made a passionate plea for us all to insource more tasks again to keep our brains fit. Ten years later, it's clear this message isn't getting through to many people. "My brain is tired. I'm happy if I can make it through the day. So the more tasks that smart apps take over from me, the better." The misconception is that people think they have to do more. My message is: the more you commit to focus, the less you actually have to work and the more time you have left for the other things in life.

I often hear CEOs declare that we need to fight the brain drain and try to hold on to as much home-grown talent as possible. Unfortunately, they are usually unaware of a much bigger brain drain in progress: in our organisations and companies, a vast amount of talent is wasted due to a lack of focus. Like Cal Newport, bestselling author of *Deep Work*, I am convinced that focus is the new IQ. No matter how smart and talented you are, if you can't focus on a given task, your entire arsenal of skills remains untapped. If we want to process complex information efficiently, concentration is crucial. If we can concentrate fully, we can finish tasks not only faster but also better. No more overtime and the accompanying chronic stress.

A proper focus on focus – pardon the pun – is not only needed in order to keep work workable and liveable, it will also be vital in order to get new employees on board. A new generation has emerged that is unwilling to work itself to death. Quiet quitting, a TikTok trend that went viral, can be seen as a silent protest from a generation that is still prepared to roll up their sleeves, but no longer at the expense of their families, friends and health. If you want to win the war for talent and attract new talent, you will first need to win the war for focus. Or that new talent will soon burn out or seek different horizons.

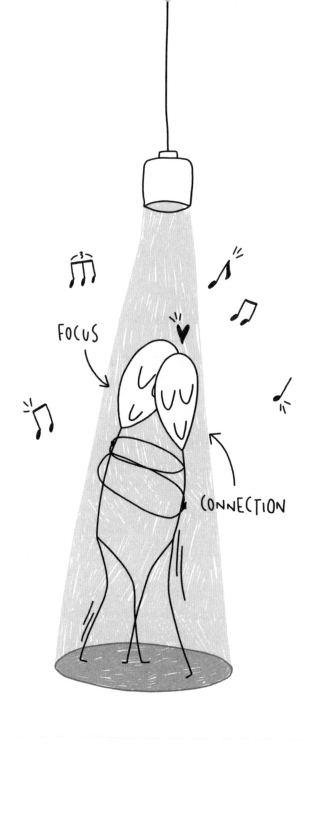

CONNECTION IS THE NEW EQ

A few months ago I received a message from a friend I hadn't seen for a long time. We had studied together, seeing each other every day, and a close friendship had developed. After graduation, we solemnly promised to continue seeing each other at least twice a year. But life happens when you're busy making other plans and meeting up regularly didn't turn out to be so easy. So when she asked if I fancied going out for a meal, I was delighted to honour our old agreement. I cleared my schedule and booked a table at a nice restaurant. It was a beautiful setting: on the waterfront, with little pleasure boats sailing by. The evening got off to a warm and friendly start. We had lots to tell each other, especially since a good deal had happened in both of our lives. I'd really been looking forward to this tête-à-tête with my friend. But what happened? At one point mid-conversation, my friend pulled out her smartphone. Not to send a message or check her socials. She simply took the phone out of her handbag and placed it on the table in front of her. To me, that felt like a real intrusion. That phone on the table shifted the atmosphere and undermined our deep connection. Should I have picked her up on it? Maybe, but her action was so spontaneous and seemed so normal that at first I didn't pay attention. It was only after a few minutes that I noticed the shift in my mood and felt quite unsettled by the phone on the table. The message seemed to be that 'something important might happen' that would instantly take precedence over our meal. And I wondered, what could be more important tonight than celebrating our friendship here in this amazing place?

It's a sign of the times. Technology constantly screams for our attention, making it increasingly difficult to truly connect with others. But we can't put all of the blame on our smartphones. If you truly want to connect, you first need to be in touch with your own goals and values. How often do you consciously make time for that? Do you ever step into your great glass elevator? Do you know what drives you and what makes you happy? Only when you have clear answers to these questions can you develop deep, authentic relationships.

Lasting connection is important not only for our personal well-being, but also for our professional durability. Together we are stronger. It's a cliché, but oh so true. If we as human beings want to set ourselves apart from artificial intelligence, we need to unite the power of our brains. Hybrid working may bring flexibility and convenience, but it also increases the risk of losing connectedness with our colleagues and loyalty to the organisation. Working from home does of course offer tremendous benefits – I'm happy too not to be stuck in traffic so often – but it's important to find a balance and make sure we stay connected to our colleagues. In a world where technology is constantly gaining ground, human connection remains the key to long-term employability and distinctiveness.

YOU'VE GOT 48 HOURS

Can I invite you to take up one last challenge? Once you've read the final page of this book, the clock starts ticking for you to put at least two of its tips into practice. For example, ask yourself regularly "what am I thinking right now?" Or fill in your attention diary for the week. Research shows that if you do nothing within the first 48 hours after acquiring new information, it quickly fades and you revert to autopilot, doing what you have always done. So if you want to break that routine, the key is to get to work, and ideally as soon as possible!

You've got 48 hours. Don't let them slip away!

Through the link below, I'd like to share some
additional online inspiration with you about focus:

https://elkegeraerts.com/focusisthenewgold

Acknowledgements

I'd like to take a moment to highlight the 'elephants' involved in the creation of this book.

Katrien Van Oost, your enthusiasm for embarking on a new book project, coupled with your remarkable ability to piece all my ideas together with precision, makes you an outstanding publisher.

Sven De Potter, many thanks for all your support and thoughtful contributions in making this book a reality. I truly enjoy working with you.

Zakaria Hammouda, it was a pleasure laying the foundations of this book with you and selecting the relevant content.

Floor Denil, your creative and associative mind translated my ideas into illustrations even before I had a chance to write them down.

My colleagues at Better Minds at Work, thank you for our brainstorming sessions on focus. I look forward to continuing this journey with you in keynotes and workshops.

Bert, thank you for all your support. I love how we bring flow into our lives as a team.

And you, dear reader, thank you for your focus!

References

In writing this book, I was able to draw on the knowledge of several esteemed colleagues and experts: Aïsha Cortoos shared her expertise on the brain, Magali De Reu guided me through the world of neurodiversity, Erik Franck confirmed the importance of self-knowledge, self-awareness and self-control, Marie Loop inspired me on how we can fully harness youthful talent and Jo Peters shared his vision of the way offices should look in the (hopefully near) future if we want to work in a more brain-friendly way.

- Abrahamsson, S. (2024), Smartphone Bans, Student Outcomes and Mental Health, NHH *Dept. of Economics Discussion Paper No. 01.*
- Ahn, J., Ahn, H. S., Cheong, J. H., & Peña, I. D. (2016). Natural Product-Derived Treatments for Attention-Deficit/Hyperactivity Disorder: Safety, Efficacy, and Therapeutic Potential of Combination Therapy. *Neural Plasticity*, 2016, 1–18.
- Bailey, C. (2020). *Hyperfocus. How to Work Less to Achieve More.* London: Pan Macmillan.
- Banbury, S., & Berry, D. C. (2005). Office noise and employee concentration: Identifying causes of disruption and potential improvements. *Ergonomics*, 48(1), 25–37.
- Baumeister, R. et al. (1995). *Losing Control. How and Why People Fail at Self-Regulation.* Cambridge, Massachusetts: Academic Press.
- Benson, H., & Proctor, W. (2004). *The Breakout Principle. How to Activate the Natural Trigger That Maximizes Creativity, Athletic Performance, Productivity, and Personal Well-Being.* New York: Simon & Schuster.
- Bernheimer, L. (2017), *The Shaping of Us. How Everyday Spaces Structure our Lives, Behaviour, and Well-Being.* London: Robinson.

- Bourdeaud'hui, H., Aesaert, K., & Van Braak, J. (2020). Identifying student- and class-level correlates of sixth-grade students' listening comprehension. *L1-Educational Studies in Language and Literature, 20*, 1–38.
- Brankele, F. (2023). *Over de kop. Wat er in je hoofd en lichaam gebeurt bij een burn-out en hoe je er weer van afkomt.* Amsterdam: Das Mag.
- Cajun Koi Academy. (2023, 21 February). *How to stay HYPER focused in a distracted world* [Video]. YouTube. https://www.youtube.com/watch?v=CgHwUONUe-0
- Cascio, J. (2010). *Human Responses to a BANI World.* Medium. Accessed via https://medium.com/@cascio/human-responses-to-a-bani-world-fb3a296e9cac
- Clear, J. (2018). *Atomic Habits. Tiny Changes, Remarkable Results.* London: Cornerstone Press.
- Compernolle, T. (2014). *Brain Chains. Discover Your Brain and Unleach Its Full Potential in a Hyperconnected Multitasking World.* Compublications: Brussels.
- Csíkszentmihályi, M. (2008). *Flow. The Psychology of Optimal Experience.* New York: Harper Perennial Modern Classics.
- De Lille, A. (2022). *Minder werken, meer doen.* Tielt: Lannoo.
- De Reu, M. (2021). *Aut of the box. Groeien & bloeien in een wereld van verschil.* Kalmthout: Pelckmans.
- De Reu, M. (2023). *Allemaal Autcasts. Wat ik nog niet wist over mijn autisme en ADHD.* Kalmthout: Pelckmans.
- Doris, R. (2023, 23 May). *Work 1 minute after waking up. it'll change your life.* [Video]. YouTube. https://www.youtube.com/watch?v=XJOsPyyYork
- Doris, R. (2023, 8 May). *How to unlock insane focus on command* [Video]. YouTube. https://www.youtube.com/watch?v=l86xggdQcKQ
- Engelbregt, H. et al. (2021). Effects of binaural and monaural beat stimulation on attention and EEG. *Experimental Brain Research, 239*(9), 2781–2791.

- Ericsson, K. A., Krampe, R., & Tesch-Römer, C. (1993). The role of deliberate practice in the acquisition of expert performance. *Psychological Review*, *100*(3), 363–406.
- Esposito, M. et al. (2021). Smart drugs and neuroenhancement: what do we know? *Frontiers in bioscience*, *26*(8), 347.
- Eyal, N. (2014). *Hooked: How to Build Habit-Forming Products*. New York: Portfolio.
- Fogg, B. J. (2020). *Tiny Habits: The Small Changes That Change Everything*. Boston: Houghton Mifflin Harcourt.
- Franck, E. (2018). *Als je niets verandert, verandert er niets*. Ghent: Borgerhoff & Lamberigts.
- Geraerts, E. (2017). *Better Minds.* How Insourcing Strengthens Resilience and Empowers Your Brain. Tielt: Lannoo.
- Geraerts, E. (2016). *Het nieuwe mentaal. Hoe lef je op weg zet naar geluk en succes*. Tielt: Lannoo.
- Geraerts, E. (2019). *Authentieke intelligentie. Waarom mensen altijd winnen van computers*. Amsterdam: Prometheus.
- Geraerts, E. (2022). *The Mental Reset.* How hybrid work and life strengthen your resilience. Tielt: Lannoo.
- Goleman, D. (2013). *The focused leader*. Harvard Business Review. Accessed via https://hbr.org/2013/12/the-focused-leader
- Grant, A. (2021). *How to stop languishing and start finding flow | TED Talk* [Video]. Accessed via https://www.youtube.com/watch?v=a3zPgyvCiJI
- Haidt, J. (2023). *The Age of Anxiety: How the Internet Is Making Us Sick and What We Can Do About It*. New York: Penguin Press.
- Hansen, A. (2023). *The Attention Fix: How to Focus in a World that Wants to Distract You*. London: Vermilion.
- Hansen, K., & Berger, C. (2011). *Speak fast, communicate well? A comparison of speech rates of television news presenters in the 1970s and today. Language & Communication*, *31*(4), 321–328.

· Hari, J. (2022). *Stolen Focus: Why You Can't Pay Attention—and How to Think Deeply Again*. New York: Crown.

· Hinssen, P. (2017). *The Day After Tomorrow: How to Survive in Times of Radical Innovation*. Leuven: LannooCampus.

· Huberman, A. & After Skool. (2023, 25 April). *How to quickly improve focus - Andrew Huberman* [Video]. YouTube. https://www.youtube.com/watch?v=_Y-7liNT1Ok

· Huberman, A. (2021, 13 September). *ADHD & How Anyone Can Improve Their Focus | Huberman Lab Podcast #37* [Video]. YouTube. https://www.youtube.com/watch?v=hFL6qRIJZ_Y

· Huberman, A. (2021, 27 September). *Controlling your dopamine for motivation, focus & satisfaction | Huberman Lab Podcast #39* [Video]. YouTube. https://www.youtube.com/watch?v=QmOFocrdyRU

· Huberman, A. (2022, 31 January). *Optimizing workspace for productivity, focus, & creativity | Huberman Lab Podcast #57* [Video]. YouTube. https://www.youtube.com/watch?v=Ze2pc6NwsHQ

· Jaucqet, C. (2024). *Trends in the Transformation Economy. Where health, well-being & happiness matter most*. Leuven: LannooCampus.

· Jiang, H., Farquharson, K., & Language and Reading Research Consortium (2018). Are working memory and behavioral attention equally important for both reading and listening comprehension? A developmental comparison. *Reading and Writing, 31*, 1449–1477.

· Kahneman, D. (2016). *Thinking, Fast and Slow*. New York: Farrar, Straus and Giroux.

· Kahneman, D., Sibony, O., & Sunstein, C.R. (2024). *Noise: A Flaw in Human Judgment*. New York: Little, Brown and Company.

· Keltner, D. (2017). *The Power Paradox: How We Gain and Lose Influence*. New York: Penguin Books.

· Kim, Y.-S., & Philips, B. (2014). Cognitive correlates of listening comprehension. *Reading Research Quarterly, 49*(3), 269–281.

- Kim, Y.-S. (2016). Direct and mediated effects of language and cognitive skills on comprehension of oral narrative texts (listening comprehension) for children. *Journal of Experimental Child Psychology, 141*, 101–120.
- Kotler, S. (2005). *The Rise of Superman. Decoding the Science of Ultimate Human Performance.* London: Quercus.
- Lai, Y., & Chang, K. (2020). Improvement of attention in elementary school students through fixation focus training activity. *International Journal of Environmental Research and Public Health, 17*(13), 4780.
- LeRoy, S. F. (2009). Why is it so hard to do my work? The challenge of attention residue when switching between work tasks. *Organizational Behavior And Human Decision Processes, 109*(2), 168–181.
- Levy, D. (2016). *Mindful Tech: How to Bring Balance to Our Digital Lives.* New Haven, Connecticut: Yale University Press.
- Loop, M. (2020). *Generatie Groei. Hoe kennis van het jonge brein de toekomst vormgeeft.* Kalmthout: Pelckmans.
- Love, J., Sung, W., & Francis, A. L. (2021). Psychophysiological responses to potentially annoying heating, ventilation, and air conditioning noise during mentally demanding work. *Journal of the Acoustical Society of America, 150*(4), 3149–3163.
- Ma, J., Ma, D., Li, Z., & Kim, H. (2021). Effects of a Workplace Sit–Stand Desk Intervention on Health and Productivity. *International Journal of Environmental Research and Public Health, 18*(21), 11604.
- Mann, S. (2016). *The Science of Boredom: Why Boredom is Good.* London: Robinson.
- Mäntylä, T. (2013). *Gender differences in multitasking reflect spatial ability. PLOS ONE, 8*(9), e79713.
- Mark, G. (2023). *Attention Span: A Novel.* New York: HarperOne.
- Meyers-Levy, J., & Zhu, R. (2007). The influence of ceiling height: the effect of priming on the type of processing that people use. *Journal of Consumer Research, 34*(2), 174–186.

- Mischel, W. et al. (1989). Delay of gratification in children. *Science,* 244(4907), 933–938.
- Nestor, J. (2020). *Breath: The New Science of a Lost Art.* New York: Riverhead Books.
- Newport, C. (2016). *Deep Work: Rules for Focused Success in a Distracted World.* New York: Grand Central Publishing.
- Norberg, J. (2017), *Progress. Ten Reasons to Look Forward to the Future.* London: OneWorld.
- Pérès, F. (2017). *Digital Detox. Minder technostress en meer focus dankzij de Touchpoints methode.* Tielt: Lannoo.
- Posner, M. I., & Petersen, S. E. (1990). The attention system of the human brain. *Annual Review of Neuroscience,* 13(1), 25–42.
- Rosen, L. D., & Gazzaley, A. (2016). *The Distracted Mind: Ancient Brains in a High-Tech World.* Cambridge, Massachussetts: MIT Press.
- Rosen, L. D., Lim, A. F., Carrier, L. M., & Cheever, N. A. (2011). *An Empirical Examination of the Educational Impact of Text Message-Induced Task Switching in the Classroom: Educational Implications and Strategies to Enhance Learning. Psychology Learning & Teaching,* 10(3), 1–12.
- Ross, B., & Lopez, M. D. (2020). 40-Hz binaural beats enhance training to mitigate the attentional blink. *Scientific Reports,* 10(1).
- S. K. L. Chang, S. K. L., & Mak, C. W. Y. (2012). *Walkability, pedestrian environment and pedestrian behaviours: A study in Hong Kong. PLOS ONE,* 7(9), e44253.
- Strayer, D. (2015). Is the Technology in Your Car Driving You to Distraction?. *Policy Insights from the Behavioral and Brain Sciences* 2(1).
- Taleb, N. N. (2012). *Antifragile: Things That Gain from Disorder.* New York: Random House.
- Tigchelaar, M. (2019). *Focus aan/uit. Dicht de 4 concentratielekken en krijg meer gedaan in een wereld vol afleiding.* Spectrum: Amsterdam.

- Touroutoglou, A., Andreano, J. M., Dickerson, B. C., & Barrett, L. F. (2020). The tenacious brain: how the anterior mid-cingulate contributes to achieving goals. *Cortex, 123,* 12–29.
- Trémolière, B., & De Neys, W. (2014). When intuitions are helpful: Prior beliefs can support reasoning in the bat-and-ball problem. *Journal of Cognitive Psychology, 26*(4):486–490.
- Van Den Bosch, C. (2024). *C-level mindset. De 7 onmisbare C-skills voor de professional van de toekomst.* Kalmthout: Pelckmans.
- Walker, M. (2017). *Why We Sleep: Unlocking the Power of Sleep and Dreams.* New York: Scribner.
- Ward, A. F., Duke, K., Gneezy, A., & Bos, M. W. (2017). *Brain Drain: The Mere Presence of One's Own Smartphone Reduces Available Cognitive Capacity. Journal of the Association for Consumer Research, 2*(2), 140–154.
- Wilson, T. et al. (2014). Just think: The challenges of the disengaged mind. *Science, 345*(6192): 75–77.
- Woollett, K., & Maguire, E. (2011). Acquiring 'the Knowledge' of London's Layout Drives Structural Brain Changes, *Current Biology, 21*(24):2109–2114.

WWW.LANNOO.COM

TRANSLATION Sue Anderson
INSIDE ILLUSTRATIONS Floor Denil
COVER DESIGN Buro Blikgoed
EDITOR Sven De Potter

© Uitgeverij Lannoo nv, Tielt, 2024 and Elke Geraerts
D/2024/45/518 – NUR 770 – ISBN 978 94 014 2917 7

All rights reserved. No part of this publication may be
reproduced, stored in a retrieval system and/or transmitted
in any form or by any means, electronic, mechanical or otherwise,
without the publisher's prior written permission.